# How to Be Calm

*How to Stop the Anxiety
and Live a Calm Life*

Amanda Hanson

ISBN: 979-8-5809-4778-5

# Table of Contents

# Introduction

Congratulations on purchasing *How to Be Calm: How to Stop the Anxiety and Live a Calm Life,* and the sincerest thank you for doing so.

The following chapters will discuss anxiety and how to deal with it so that you can live a life of peace and calm. Anxiety comes in many different forms and will cause you to react in many different ways. The one thing that is true about all forms of anxiety is that anxiety will ruin your life. This fear does not refer to the usual amount of tension people feel before going on a first or date taking a big test. This fear comes from the kind of anxiety that makes you sweat profusely, stammer and stutter, and tremble uncontrollably. This issue is the kind of fear that keeps you from meeting new people, experiencing new events, and living your life to its fullest potential. When anxiety takes over and robs you of the primary pleasures every human has the right to enjoy, then the pressure needs to go.

But saying you want to be less anxious and doing it might be two different things. Maybe you don't know what is causing your anxiety. Perhaps you don't understand why you feel uneasy. Perhaps you do know these answers, but you don't know what to do about it. Everyone desires a beautiful life. You might imagine this time will be different, that this time you will find your safe place. You will let go of your anxiety and feel full of joy and security. Then something triggers memories of bad things buried in the past, or you thought they were buried in the past, and bring them to the front of your mind. It won't if the buried memory happened last year or twenty years ago; it is still there in your subconscious, taunting you and your desire for happiness. And then you begin that downward slide into anxiety so deep and so thick that it threatens the joy and happiness you hoped would save you from any further stress.

You will never truly enjoy a happy life until you learn to let go of the past events that haunt you, that creep back into your conscious mind and fill you with dread. The source of the anxiety is not as important as learning to deal with it. You have elements in your past that are clouding your future. Now is your time to put them in the past where they belong and leave them there. Now is your time for you to live your life free of anxiety and the guilt and shame that go along with those feelings. Using this book, you will see how to identify the triggers that bring on your pressure and how to eliminate them. Suppression no longer works, as you have probably discovered. Getting rid of the feelings surrounding those past events will get rid of your anxiety and allow you to live with peace and calm.

There are numerous helpful books on this subject on the market; thank you again for choosing this one! Every effort has been taken to make sure that it is full of as much useful information as possible; please enjoy!

# Chapter 1: Anxiety Can Ruin Your Life

Anxiety is the reaction that your mind and experience when you face an unfamiliar, dangerous, or stressful situation in any way. Stress itself is not a destructive emotion. A certain amount of anxiety will keep you aware of what is around you and alert you to anything that might happen. Feelings of stress are just another part of the process of being a human. Anxiety and fear are natural responses to the danger that is anticipated realistically. This anticipation makes anxiety just another survival technique that you need to keep you safe in this world. It is necessary for specific situations. If someone is physically threatening you, if an animal is responding viciously or if there is a fire, these are all situations where you might feel anxious, and you should. These are all threats that could harm you, so in feeling anxiety, you will be prompted to fight to save yourself or to run away from the danger – the fight or flight syndrome. This reaction is necessary if people are to survive in this world.

Anxiety is an emotion that is born from fear. You feel fear when you are confronted with a situation. You feel pressure when you fear the absence of any real problem or when the issue is different. Suppose a doctor once mistreated you, and you felt fear during the encounter. In that case, you might feel anxiety whenever you see a doctor or think of going to the doctor, even though the current situation has nothing to do with your original fear. Anxiety may appear in conditions that have nothing to do with the things you have experienced. If you regularly watch crime dramas or horror movies, then you might feel anxious if you are forced to come home alone late at night or if you find yourself on a dark street alone. There is probably no real danger in either of these situations, but your mind feels there might be, so you react by feeling anxiety.

## Physical Signs of Anxiety

While the triggers for the various types of anxiety disorders may differ, they all share one commonality, and that is the distinct potential to cause you to feel physical symptoms born of anxiety. The feelings manifest in your body in multiple ways no matter  whether you are dealing with mild anxiety or a diagnosed anxiety disorder. The natural release of stress hormones will impact almost every system in your body. Your innate fight-or-flight response is the cause of your physical symptoms of anxiety. Typically, this response is there to ensure you survive a threat by fighting off the threat or escaping. When your ancestors lived in caves, that threat might have been a vicious lion or a flood. With anxiety, the threat to you is the worry and fear you feel. Your sympathetic nervous system is elevated to kick into high gear while controlling processes that are involuntary like your inhalation and heart rate. This perceived threat spurs the secretion from the adrenal glands to emit hormones such as cortisol and adrenaline.

This reaction is a definite sign of anxiety because the rate of your heart is controlled by your sympathetic nervous system. When dealing with stress and your body churns out hormones, your heart reacts by beating faster. This speed enables your heart to send extra blood flowing to your larger muscles so you are able to either flee or fight off a threat. But when your foe is anxiety, a heart racing will heighten your nerves even more. Your heart pumps to circulate oxygen around your body. The breathing will also elevate to give your body with even more oxygen. Your response to stress elevates the speed at which you are sending blood flowing around through your body. If you breathe too fast, a syndrome that is known as hyperventilation, you might enhance many of the symptoms of physical anxiety because your oxygen-carbon dioxide levels become imbalanced.

A common sign of anxiety is a persistent feeling of fatigue for two crucial reasons. The increase in the flow of stress hormones caused by the rise in pressure can keep your body elevated up on high alert, which can definitely drain your energy. The other reason is based on the fact that anxiety and sleep have a strange relationship.

When you suffer from anxiety, you might have trouble falling asleep or remaining asleep. Your sleep might be disturbed and unfulfilling. When your hormone levels are elevated, you might find it difficult to sleep well. Your body needs to relax to rest but it is buzzing with all of these extra hormones and feelings. Anxiety brings wildly racing thoughts that are no recipe for great sleep, either. And when sleep problems cause you to have insomnia, which is one more thing to add to the list of items that cause anxiety.

Your muscles will answer stress by tightening. When you hold various parts of your body in a rigid position for extended time periods, you will feel pain. Anxiety will often lead to tightness in the neck or along your back and shoulders. Some people will also tightly clench their jaw or feel the tightness in their muscles up into their head, leading to headaches. Anxiety is also problematic in your gastrointestinal system. People suffering with anxiety may often notice general stomach issues like diarrhea, pain, constipation, or other kinds of gastrointestinal distress. Part of this is because your mind controls your stomach and all of the stress hormones your body has been releasing. Digestion can be affected by poor lifestyle choices caused by anxiety-like not exercising regularly or eating poorly. When you are fighting with fear, the thought of sweating profusely might make it worse. Unfortunately, excessive profuse sweating is a commonly annoying side effect of many disorders caused by anxiety. When the symptoms of anxiety overwhelm your nervous system, it can influence the sweat glands found all over your body.

If you have ever trembled violently from fear before a big event, you have seen how your body reacts when it is under pressure. This trembling is the same reaction your body has to anxiety-induced hormone surges. Anxiety is usually caused by trying to anticipate unknown threats. Always being on guard will make you startle more easily.

You might even find that you have problems with swallowing. Anxiety might cause tightness in your throat since you might feel like something is stuck there. This feeling can make anxiety feel even worse. Especially in high anxiety periods, many people who suffer from anxiety tend to get sick more often. Your immune system will function poorly when anxiety levels are high for too long. This syndrome might cause you to be much more susceptible to catching viruses like the common cold.

## Emotional Signs of Anxiety

Anxiety causes many emotional responses because it is an emotional-based disorder. Anxiety is a real emotion, even if many people feel it is not, so there is no need to deny that emotional responses from anxiety are very real. You might experience other emotions that are caused by anxiety like irritation, feeling sad, and anger. Feeling anxiety is a state of emotion by itself, and you will be more likely to suffer from these dynamic mood swings and living your life with a general loss of happiness.

Feeling anxiety will expose you to an enormous amount of stress that will make you feel even more anxious. A little bit of pressure now and then can have its benefits. Anxiety will let you know when you need changes in your life and you need to do some things differently. Small bits of stress are good for you, because they let you know that you need to avoid dark alleys, drive safely, or work extra hours to make the deadline for a project. When that anxiety becomes chronic or overwhelming, it becomes a real problem. Long-term stress changes the balance of chemicals that are present in your brain, the ones that balance and affect the levels of your emotions. Most of the changes that anxiety will make to your mind are the exact same changes that will happen when you experience an event full of sadness.

The issue will become more chronic as your brain becomes adapted to these levels. It is unclear why your brain adapts or how, but prolonged anxiety will cause issues with your mental health that might last for the long term.

In many ways, stress and anxiety relate directly to each other. While technically they are different kinds of conditions, many of the same problems are shared by both. Having stress about an event will cause anxiety, and when you feel anxiety it will cause you to feel stress. Since fear is related to your fight/flight system, anxiety has other effects, like releasing adrenaline. Still, it can also lead to feelings of stress, and stress will lead you to having trouble with happiness and controlling your emotions. It is sometimes hard to tell what symptoms are caused by anxiety and what symptoms are caused by pressure stress since the two are so closely related. Regardless, it's clear that stress plays a crucial role in the development of poor emotional regulation.

Emotional responses that are caused by anxiety are much more complicated because all of your emotions are complicated. Emotional fatigue can also be one of the causes of anxiety. Dealing with panic attacks and anxiety on a daily basis can be exhausting. It is not unusual for people to constantly feel irritated or numb when they are forced to deal with the symptoms of anxiety on a regular basis.

The emotions that are caused by intense anxiety can be complicated and will cause great upset. You might often feel like you are the only one who ever feel this way because it is stressful to deal with those emotional responses regularly.

Many people experience anxiety attacks or deal with chronic anxiety, and these issues will cause their own set of emotions, and the compilation of these negative thoughts and feelings can lead to even further emotional issues. Stress comes from the result of poor coping abilities with mental issues. When you have poor skills with coping, it will also create problems for you in trying to control other types of negative emotions, such as sadness and irritation. When you face some adverse event or feeling and have problems coping with your anxiety and emotions, you might have a more challenging time holding your negative emotions in check.

## Origins of Anxiety

Many factors can cause anxiety. Many causes of adult anxiety begin in your childhood. Having a close family member who is abusive or neglectful, or addicted to a substance can cause a child to be anxious and fearful. If the parents have control over every aspect of their child's life and don't teach them to be autonomous, they will never learn to develop life skills. If the parents themselves have anxiety disorders, it is more likely that they will have anxiety disorders. When people experience chronic stress of stressful events in life, they will likely develop anxiety disorders. These events might be emotional, sexual, or physical abuse; extreme poverty, loss of a parent or sibling, separation from a loved one, or even your physical illness or that of a family member can cause mental and emotional trauma that will turn itself into relationship anxiety in adulthood.

Specific physical characteristics can make a person more prone to experiencing real or imagined fears that lead to adult anxiety. Being a woman and trying to compete in more male-oriented jobs, being a compassionate man, being a person of color, or being a person from a different culture or nationality, all of these are situations that can cause feelings of anxiety.

Sometimes the cause of anxiety does not begin until adulthood. Many people who enjoy relatively normal and happy childhoods can suffer from adulthood events that will lead to stress. These are similar to the events that cause stress in children, such as abuse of any kind, divorce or domestic violence, family issues, money problems, and inadequacy feelings.

Children and adults alike can suffer from social anxiety issues that can lead to anxiety in their lives, and these feelings often present themselves as relationship anxiety. Things like parties and other large gatherings where some people are strangers, unfavorable interactions with authority figures, meeting new people and dating, public speaking, and speaking to strangers in any situation.

Anxiety is a part of everyday life, and some stress is good for you. The tension that causes you to adhere to extreme routines puts a wedge between you and those important to you or disturbs your life's regular pattern; this type of anxiety is not typical and will need to be addressed.

# Chapter 2: Anxiety Disorders

Occasional anxiety is normal, but the anxiety that is caused by disorders are different. These are a collection of mental illnesses that cause constant and overwhelming fear and anxiety. Excessive stress can make you avoid school, work, family gatherings, and other social situations that might trigger or worsen your symptoms. Anxiety disorders are not the same as normal feelings of anxiety or nerves.

Fear is the present anticipation of a concern about future events and is associated more with tension in the muscles and trying to avoid certain behaviors. An attack of anxiety is the emotional response given to a threat that is imagined or real. It is more often associated with the fight or flight reaction. Anxieties disorders can make you avoid situations that will trigger their symptoms or make them worse. Schoolwork, job performance, and personal relationships can all be affected. Anxiety disorders come with many names like separation anxiety disorder, agoraphobia, anxiety disorder of a social nature, and generalized anxiety disorder.

## Generalized Anxiety Disorder

Constant, unfounded, and excessive worry about several different things characterizes Generalized Anxiety Disorder (GAD). People who suffer from

GAD may always expect disaster. They are often overly concerned with matters revolving around health, family, money, or work. It is difficult to control this worry. These people will worry when there is no apparent cause for concern or why the person will disturb more than necessary.

Sometimes just waking up and thinking of getting through the day produces anxiety. The constant cycle of worry never ends, and people feel the concern is beyond their control. Even knowing rationally that the fear you feel is overly intense for the situation at hand, they cannot stop worrying. Many of the people with GAD will try to plan or be in control of all situations. This may be because most of the disorders related to anxiety related to a difficulty with tolerating uncertainty. Some people truly believe that constant worry will prevent terrible events from happening, so to them it is risky to let go of their concern. GAD can even cause struggles with physical symptoms such as headaches and stomachaches.

People who are diagnosed with this disorder can still function socially. They can be gainfully employed and live happy lives. As long as their anxiety levels are in the mild to moderate range, or those levels are responding to treatment, they will function just fine. They will often avoid certain situations because of the disorder they have, or they may not take full advantage of the opportunities they are able to because of their excessive worry. Carrying through with some of the simplest daily activities will be difficult for some people who can't get past their excessive worry. .

Generalized anxiety disorder symptoms can vary. They may include:

- Fear of making the wrong decision or general indecisiveness
- Persistent worrying or anxiety about many areas that are out of proportion
- to the impact of the events
- Difficulty concentrating on one particular task
- Including solutions to all possible outcomes and overthinking plans
- Continually feeling on edge, keyed up, or unable to relax
- Imagining potential threats in every event or situation
- Holding on to unnamed worry and not able to let go
- Difficulty handling uncertainty

Physical signs and symptoms may include:

- Irritability
- Fatigue
- Nausea, diarrhea, or irritable bowel syndrome
- Trouble sleeping

- Sweating
- Muscle tension or muscle aches
- Nervousness or being easily startled
- Trembling, feeling twitchy

You might still feel anxious for no apparent reason, sometimes even if your worry does not consume you. For example, you may have a general sense that something terrible is about to happen, or you may feel intense concern about your safety or that of your loved ones. You might have problems at work or in social situations because of your constant anxiety. Your worries might shift from one concern to another, and they may change with age and time.

## Separation Anxiety Disorder

When someone fears being kept away from a certain place, person, or sometimes even a belonging or a pet, they have the anxiety disorder known as separation anxiety disorder. Think of the toddler who can't go anywhere without his blanket. Separation anxiety is usually associated with young children, but adults will often experience this condition too. It is a normal phenomenon in small children. Separation anxiety in an adult can come from many sources of separation. Sometimes this form of anxiety will appear as the symptom of another type of mental illness. These extreme symptoms may also include delusions stemming from psychotic types of disorders or fearing change in their routine, such as a disorder on the autism spectrum.

Adults who are controlling or overly protective might be considered to have separation anxiety disorder, but this behavior stems from their desire to keep those close to them safe and free from being hurt.

If separation anxiety continues into adulthood, it is called adult separation anxiety disorder. Separation anxiety in children is often associated with extreme fear or worry about being away from parents or caregivers. These children are usually not willing to participate in events or social experiences.  They are not willing to spend the night at a friend's house or go away to summer sleepaway camp. In adulthood, the anxiety is around being away from children or spouses. Children who suffer from separation anxiety may do poorly in school. For adults, the impairment may lead to poor work performance or the inability to be part of a meaningful relationship.

Being stressed about the health and safety of friends and family is normal. The high anxiety levels and sometimes even panic attacks when loved ones are out of reach that adults experience is not typical. These people may be socially withdrawn or show extreme sadness or difficulty concentrating when away from loved ones. As parents, the condition might lead to a parenting style that is strict and overly involved with the children. You might be an overbearing partner in your personal relationships.

There are other common symptoms of separation anxiety:

- Anxiety attacks or depression related to any of the above topics
- unfounded and unnecessary fears that someone you love will be abducted or fatally injured
- difficulty or inability to sleep away from loved ones because you fear that something might happen to them if you are not there
- constant refusal or hesitancy to leave the general area of loved ones

This disorder might also cause physical aches and pains, headaches, and diarrhea associated with periods of anxiety.

## Obsessive-Compulsive Disorder

When people suffer from the constant desire to act out a routine to avoid feeling worry over certain situations, this is known as obsessive compulsive disorder, or OCD. Repetitive types of behaviors like these, such as checking on things, washing their hands repeatedly or cleaning something that is already clean, can definitely interfere with regular social interactions and daily activities.

OCD is different from having a routine to accomplish certain tasks in a specific order. Many people prioritize the tasks in their daily life so they fall into a routine that is easy to remember. With OCD, the person will experience significant distress if they do not perform these routines, even though the patterns and behaviors are rigid. Some of the people with OCD will suspect or know the obsessions they have are not real or they may freely acknowledge their obsessions as reality. Even when these people know their obsessive habits are not natural, people who have OCD have difficulty focusing on the task at hand. Their minds want to return to the compulsive actions and focus on the obsession.

An obsession is a persistently recurring impulse, thought, or image that causes feelings of distress such as anxiety or fear. Many of the people who have OCD will recognize that the urges, beliefs, or ideas they have are produced by their mind, and they will know these thoughts are unreasonable and excessive. These thoughts are intrusive and are not stopped by reason or logic. OCD makes people try to suppress their obsessions or try to ignore them or substitute them with another action or thought. Common OCD habits include worrying excessively about germs and dirt, the need to keep objects in straight lines or exact patterns, or focusing excessively on religious beliefs or sexual preferences that are normally forbidden.

When someone feels the need to constantly repeat a certain act in response to something that is worrying them, then that is a compulsion. The actions are used for reducing stress in a feared situation or ultimately preventing it from happening. Constantly repeating certain rituals may fill the day in the most severe cases, making a routine impossible. Knowing that these rituals are irrational will only compound that anguish. However, the compulsion may temporarily bring relief from the constant worry; but when the obsession comes back, the cycle will continue to happen.

Some examples of compulsions:

- Striving to reduce the fear of harming oneself or others by, for example, developing a ritual to make sure the refrigerator is closed. Sometimes people will retrace driving routes repeatedly to make certain they haven't run over anyone.
- Mental compulsions respond to obsessive intrusive thoughts; some say words or phrases or pray to lower their anxiety or keep away the occurrence of a future event they dread might happen.

- They will spend many hours cleaning areas that are already clean to make sure no germs or dirt is left behind to contaminate them. Many hours might be devoted to washing or cleaning their surroundings.
- Ordering and arranging items to reduce discomfort. Certain items need to be in a particular order, and items might need to be lined up in a row or be symmetric.
- They will repeat someone's name or a certain phrase several times in a row. Their intelligent mind tells them that this will not save them from harm, but their emotional mind tells them this is needed to feel safe.

## Agoraphobia

When people suffer from this anxiety disorder they fear feeling helpless or threatened in a public place, or they feel they might be embarrassed accidentally. These people fear everyday activities and try to avoid being in an open space outside, riding on public transportation, crossing over a bridge, or being caught helpless in crowds like what happens in shopping areas or concerts. If the disorder becomes strong enough they will be afraid to leave home.

There are specific events that can increase the probability that someone will develop agoraphobia. These events include being attacked, experiencing any kind of abuse, or suffering the death of someone they are close to. People who are naturally high-strung individuals or who have a family history of the disorder will have a higher risk of developing agoraphobia. Those people who have agoraphobia will feel stress or anxiety when they recall an occasion where they were. They will also feat being in those situations where they might not be able to get help when needed. The situation might feel threatening to their safety when they leave their house. They will avoid those situations that might trigger these feelings.

Agoraphobia also includes certain physical symptoms:

- Fear of dying
- Rapid heart rate
- Chest pain or pressure
-
- Feeling a loss of control
- Excessive sweating
- Upset stomach or diarrhea
- Trouble breathing
- Sudden flushing or chills
- Lightheadedness or dizziness
- Shakiness, numbness, or tingling

# Social Anxiety Disorder

This disorder is marked by the intense fear of being rejected in public. Fearing being judged or evaluated in a negative manner is also known as social phobia. These people might worry about acting or appearing visibly anxious. They are embarrassed by their own blushing or stuttering, or they feel others view them as awkward, stupid, or boring. Sufferers will often avoid social situations or performance situations because of the social anxiety. They can experience significant anxiety and distress if a problem cannot be avoided. Intense physical symptoms are experienced by many people with a social anxiety disorder. They might feel sweaty, have an increased heart rate, or feel sick to their stomach. If they find themselves in a situation that they fear then they might suffer a full panic attack. Although they know that their fear is excessive and unreasonable, people with social anxiety disorder usually feel completely powerless against their anxiety.

This disorder can completely disrupt the lives of those who suffer from it. They may decline to take part in any activity that puts them around other people. They avoid social situations for fear they might have problems around other people. Their daily lives may be disrupted if the symptoms are severe enough. They might interfere greatly with occupational performance, regular routines, or the chance to enjoy a social life. Any form of regular activity that others take for granted are excruciating for people with this disorder if they involve being around other people. These people are also more likely to develop chemical dependencies and depression.

## Post-Traumatic Stress Disorder (PTSD)

This disorder occurs in people who have seen or experienced an event they found to be traumatic. This can be anything from an accident, a natural occurrence or disaster, an act of war, live combat or they have been a victim of rape. It also affects those people who have been threatened with any form of violence or death or severe injury.

PTSD was known by many different names in the past, such as shell shock or combat fatigue, but veterans of combat are not the only victims. PTSD can happen to anyone.

The traumatic event causes emotional responses that linger long after the event is over. They might relive the event by having flashbacks or nightmares. They might experience feelings of intense anger or sadness or fear. They might never be able to feel attached to anyone else. Anything that reminds them of the traumatic event is something to be avoided. Any loud noise or accidental touch is enough to elicit a response from them.

Diagnosing PTSD will require the person was exposed to an event. The event might not be one that they were involved in, but it can be one they were witness to, such as hearing the story of a loved one telling about a trauma or a police officer working a case.

Symptoms of PTSD fall into four categories. Specific symptoms can vary in severity.

- Alterations in thought and mood: The person might not be able to recall the details of the event. They may feel negative feelings and thoughts that lead to ongoing beliefs about them or others that are distorted or incomplete. They may incorrectly place blame because their memory of the event is distorted. They might also feel unending feelings of shame, guilt, anger, and fear that leaves them unable to enjoy events or becoming attached to others.
- They might avoid reminders of the traumatic event that may trigger distressing memories, including avoiding anything that would remind them of it. People may try to avoid reminders. They will often refuse to discuss their feelings about the event or what happened.
- They may engage in self-destructive behaviors. They may irritate easily or be suspicious of others. They usually struggle

to concentrate for long periods and have issues with sleeping well.

- As much as they try to bury the event in their subconscious, it will reappear when they least expect it.

PTSD often happens with other anxiety disorders. It is diagnosed when the symptoms last for more than a short time and cause many instances of stress and anxiety in the person's life.

## Panic Disorder

This disorder is characterized by massive waves of fear that cause the person to be unable tom function. You can't breathe and your heart pounds. These attacks can happen with no real reason and at any time or place. These attacks can happen at any time, even when the person is sleeping.

Panic attacks can happen just once, although that is usually not the case. Specific situations will cause attacks to happen over and over again. An episode is more likely to happen if the person has already had an episode in the same situation. You feel trapped with no real escape, and that feeling will trigger your flight or fight response to kick in.

People who are otherwise happy and healthy can have panic attacks. Having another anxiety disorder might trigger episodes. Panic attacks are treatable regardless of the cause. You can control the events in your life by using different strategies that will help you eliminate the occurrences.

The signs and symptoms can develop abruptly and will usually peak within a few minutes. Most attacks will end within twenty to thirty minutes and most will last less than an hour. They will happen at any time and in any place. You might have an attack while driving, shopping, relaxing, or even sleeping.

Some of the symptoms might include:

- Fear of losing control, dying or going crazy
- Nausea or upset stomach
- Heart palpitations or racing heart
- Numbness or tingling sensations
- Feeling dizzy, light-headed, or faint
- Trembling or shaking
- Choking feeling
- Chest pain or discomfort
- Shortness of breath or hyperventilation
- Sweating
- Feeling unreal or detached from your surroundings
- Hot or cold flashes

Since many of the symptoms are physical in nature, many people think they are having a heart attack. People suffering from a panic attack often go to the emergency room for treatment. While it is important to rule out possible physical medical causes of symptoms, panic is usually overlooked as a cause of the physical symptoms.

Those people who suffer from more than two panic attacks regularly each week may have developed panic disorder. Suffering repeated panic attacks, is the primary characteristic of this disorder, combined with significant behavior changes or the intense fear of having further attacks.

You may have the panic disorder if you:

- Avoid places where you have had a previous attack out of fear of the place itself
- Worry about having another panic attack
- Frequently experience attacks that aren't related to a specific situation

The experience of having a panic attack can leave lasting impressions, even if the attack only lasts a few minutes. You might suffer a serious emotional toll if you have more than one attack. A lasting memory is left by the feelings of terror and fear you felt. Your self-confidence might be impacted negatively and your everyday life might be severely disrupted. This can eventually lead to the following symptoms of panic disorder:

Anticipating attacks of anxiety – you feel anxious and tense between panic attacks and never quite feel relaxed and more like your usual self. Feeling fear that you might have future panic attacks will lead to this fear. This fear of being afraid never quite goes away and can disable you from daily events.

Developing phobias to avoid things – You begin to avoid specific environments and situations. You might believe that you can avoid the problem caused by previous attacks. You fear the occurrence of an attack so you avoid specific places and events. In the extreme version, this type of avoidance of the phobia triggers can turn into agoraphobia.

Remember that disorders involving anxiety are quite different from normal anxiety. Normal anxiety is part of everyday life, and a little bit can be useful for you. Anxiety disorders can bring your life to a halt, and they are the most prevalent form of illness of a mental variety. Everyday stress does not cause the same levels of anxiety that disorders do. Specific situations might cause you to feel irrational fears or intense physical symptoms.

# Chapter 3: Causes Of Anxiety

No one wakes up one day, suddenly feeling anxious where they have never felt nervous before. The fears that eventually become anxieties usually have their root in childhood, and they are caused by things that occur in a child's life. These events may or may not be typical, everyday events. Still, for whatever reason, they become lodged in the child's memory banks to reappear in the future adult and cause anxiety.

Being a child is an anxious process all by itself, without the outside world butting in. From birth, children spend their days overcoming fears, mastering new challenges, and learning new skills. They are tasked with navigating a world that often makes no sense to them. Children have small things that stress m and cause them fears, and most of the time, a caring adult can make everything better with a hug and smile. Some children do not have the luxury of a happy home or a loving parent, and for them, the stress of childhood events is never alleviated. These children generally grow up to have some type of anxiety disorder, as the known fears of youth become the imagined fears of adulthood. Sometimes children's lives are filled with traumatic events that are impossible for them to handle. When this happens, these stresses from childhood are carried over into adulthood.

Different childhood events will have different outcomes for the adult, but all will somehow cloud the adult's emotions.

## Emotionally Distant Parents

Having an emotionally unavailable parent can scar a child for life and lead to real problems in their adulthood. When parents are too emotionally detached, they will exhibit many different behavior types toward their children. They may always seek their child's attention or others around them; they might engage in harmful behaviors or indulge in unstable relationships, have trouble setting reasonable boundaries for their child and act aggressively toward the child. They have a low tolerance for the stresses that come with raising a child.

Children who grow up with emotionally distant parents will suffer from emotional problems as adults. As adults, these people will have developed characteristics to protect themselves. Their struggle with forming meaningful relationships might lead them into a series of short-term, unfulfilling relationships. They may fear deep love and emotional attachment because they highlight their deficiencies and inability to commit to real love. They may also be incredibly selfish people, trying to make up for what they did not get in their childhood attachments. They will suffer from anxiety

because they know they don't have what it takes
to form real, meaningful relationships.

## Death or Abandonment

Whether a child is left alone by abandonment or
by a parent's death, both can affect the adult the
child will become. Children naturally become
emotionally attached to the people who take care
of them, and when those people are no longer in
their lives, the child feels hurt and confused.
Children learn to form close bonds with other
people when they become attached to their
caretakers. When these people leave, the child's
ability to develop essential relationships can be
permanently damaged.

These same feelings will follow the person into
adulthood. Abandonment, as a child, can leave
an adult struggling with feelings of
unworthiness, low self-esteem, an unreasonable
desire for perfection, and a constant desire to
avoid conflict at all costs. As adults, these people
will often give in on important issues to avoid
conflict with their partner. And they may try to
create the perfect relationship to eliminate the
possibility that their partner might abandon
them, which will also fill them with feelings of
failure and inadequacy.

The long-term emotional effects of childhood trauma can scar an adult for life. The things we learn about ourselves in childhood, whether real or not, will carry into adulthood. Our beliefs and ideas will mold the way we see our relationships and see ourselves in the relationship. And if we are left with only negative emotions from childhood, then that is what we will carry into our adult relationships.

It is possible to change what you have learned and how you see yourself as an adult. When you discover just where your anxiety is coming from, you can work to overcome the feelings that make you anxious and quell the fear that makes you behave in a certain way. You will need to know where the issue started in your childhood so that you can plot a path to recovery. As an adult, you can conquer the childhood fears that currently overwhelm your life and work to eliminate them.

## Residential Instability

Some children are not able to grow up in one house their entire lives. Sometimes moving is inevitable, especially in homes where the employer is a branch of the military or one parent is pursuing an advanced field of study. The constant moving that causes stress and trauma to children, and eventual anxiety to their adult selves, is the kind of moving that can be attributed to negative reasons. Children who are forced to move are the children who will suffer from being forced to move continuously. Sometimes the cause is not the parent's fault, such as one parent lost their job, there is a drop in the family's income level, parents separate or divorce or remarry, or when illegal activity is involved.

These children never have the advantage of feeling safe and secure in one living space since they never know when they might be forced to move again. Their schoolwork will probably suffer since they will never be in one place long enough to retain any learning amount. They eventually stop trying to develop friendships, knowing that they will soon leave this place and these people for a new home with new faces. This constant moving around will affect their social skills and their ability to feel successful as an adult. They will likely be behind their peers in social and academic skills.

As adults, these people will know full well that they are slightly inferior to the people around them. There will be life skills that they never learned, and this will cause them great anxiety when they begin to navigate the adult world. They will anticipate future situations that they know will stress them because they will not be successful in those situations. Trying to avoid these situations will bring them even more anxiety.

## Overly Critical Parents and Guardians

The overly critical parent and the smothering parent are often the same people; two entities in one, and neither are any good for the child's mental health. The overly critical parent may have the child's best interests in mind when they continuously push their children to excel at everything and achieve more, but this can also lead to adult anxiety.

Children can be challenging themselves. There is always the drive to be better among children than the kid next to them to come first to one-up everyone else. When a child is continuously criticized by the adults in their lives and told they aren't good enough, they will eventually believe the parent's negative words. They will begin to use those negative thoughts to explain away all of the wrong or adverse events in their lives. If they aren't invited to a party or they do poorly on a school assignment, it must be because they aren't good enough. As adults, they will struggle with self-esteem problems and feelings of inadequacy. Any time that they feel they won't measure up, they will begin to feel anxiety. As adults, these people will be highly critical of their efforts while at the same time trying to avoid situations where they might be judged on their inadequacies. The idea that they may not measure up to their partner's expectations will cause them great anxiety.

# Helicopter Parents

We've all heard the term 'helicopter parent,' and we all know someone who fits that description. This parent is the one who stands over their children until all of their homework is entirely complete, the parent who spends most of their time directing their child's behavior with commands to 'stand up straight' and 'fix your hair.' This type of parent has no time for themselves because they are so busy ferrying their children to one activity after another. This is the helicopter parent, and they are so busy arranging every little detail of their children's lives that they cannot see how they are smothering their children.

Children who grow up with parents who smother them will enter adulthood as stunted individuals. These adults will suffer from a maladjusted view of perfectionism. They will feel that they need to be perfect in all things while at the same time, knowing that they will never achieve the level of perfection that will make themselves and others truly happy. These adults will be more depressed, self-critical, and anxious because of this. Not only will these adults feel that they will never be good enough in their accomplishments, but they will also fear being left to their own devices for too long. They desperately want to please their partner, but they can't see themselves as separate from their partner for too long. And since they never learned to experience failure and all of the emotions that go along with it, they fear failure and develop ways to avoid it. This brings another level of anxiety as they struggle to be happy and try to live somewhat normally.

## Childhood Shyness

Some shyness in children is quite usual. Children have not experienced all of the situations that are possible to share, and so they will always be faced with events that are new and unfamiliar to them. When the child's fear of social interaction is severe and not addressed in childhood, that individual may grow up to experience severe social anxiety. Shyness is nothing more than cautiousness in the face of a new experience. Social anxiety is the inability to develop and grow socially or to function in a social setting. These adults will find it challenging to build and retain meaningful social relationships, leading to even more anxiety and depression. When the adult knows they lack social skills, they will feel anxious when faced with a situation where they need to be sociable. They will build a life driven by their anxiety when they need to be out in society and make every effort to avoid social situations. They will eventually feel anxious, just thinking about being sociable. This shyness can affect every part of their adult life, from intimate relationships to their careers. People who feel this level of social anxiety will have actual physical symptoms when they are forced to be in public.

## Childhood Poverty

One determiner of mental health is poverty. It profoundly influences other aspects of a person's life, like their health, social standing, community conditions, and self-esteem. The long-range impact of poverty on a person's mental health can potentially reach across the entire span of their lives. Children who grow up as victims of extreme poverty often lack many opportunities to guarantee a good experience as adults. These children usually perform poorly in school and have more behavioral issues.

Children who grow up in poverty-stricken urban areas may suffer deficiencies in social settings. The places they grow up in are less like neighborhoods and more like war zones that need to be navigated daily. People may look at one another with mistrust and may go out of their way to avoid other people. These children see life as a constant battle, something to be fought and won. Or they go with the flow and become resigned to their fate. Either reaction will cloud their vision of life as an adult and can lead to adult anxieties.

When children grow up in poverty and accept poverty as a way of life, they will be less likely to rise above poverty as adults. They will be complacent and may seem to be unambitious and even lazy. These children grow into adulthood with their own set of anxieties. Used to doing without, they will feel stressed if anyone pushes them to be more than they think they can be. They will retreat into the shell of complaisance that has protected them all of their lives at any moment they believe that they are or might be pressured to accomplish more than they think is possible. If they expect nothing, they will not be disappointed, and expecting more will cause them to feel stress.

Children who think the other way, those who see poverty as something to overcome will grow into adults who feel the need to succeed at everything they attempt. They will not take 'no' for an answer, and they will stop at nothing to get what they want. This intensity brings them their unique type of adult anxiety. A failure is never an option, and they will not stop in their quest for success. They will anticipate future situations that will make them feel as though they might not be successful, leading to anxiety. They will feel anxious and stressed if they fail the first time.

## Teachers and Other Authority Figures

Children who struggle to pay attention in the classroom and are restless are usually diagnosed with an attention-related disorder, but the cause might be simple anxiety. Kids who are anxious in the classroom might not separate their worries from their conscious thinking long enough to retain meaningful learning. And they might have moments of clarity that are overtaken by feelings of anxiety that will make them seem to drift away again. Their behavior is triggered by stress, but it may look like they are not paying attention.

Children who struggle with separation anxiety might also have problems leaving the house long enough to go to school. To stay home and enjoy a bit of parental attention, they might pretend to be sick. This anxiety could be because they do not want to be away from their parents. It might also be that the children are trying to avoid going to school.

Acting aggressively, or acting out, might not be symptoms that are typically associated with anxiety. Still, in children, both of these may be signs that the child struggles with issues more extensive than what they can handle along. Children who feel anxious may rebel if the schedule is changed without warning or if another child is not following the rules. Anxiety can also make children show signs of aggression. Because they cannot make sense of their inner feelings, they will act out in external ways.

Some children do well on school tests but seem to disappear into the walls when it is time for class discussions. Children who might be eager to show off their skills, who are comfortable with their abilities, will let the teacher know in some way that they want to be called on. But the anxious child will never raise their hand or make eye contact when the teacher is looking for volunteers; they will pretend to be working busily on nothing at all, and if they are called on, they may freeze and not be able to answer the question. And frequent absences for illness or frequent trips to the school nurse may be another sign of childhood school-related anxiety.

Students who suffer from performance anxiety, the need to be perfect in all things, might also do poorly in school. These children are obsessed with perfection and will stop at nothing to achieve it, whether excellent attendance, perfect grades or joining all of the available extracurricular programs; they will settle for nothing less than ideal. They may achieve perfection at the cost of their happiness, and if they do not reach the success, they will feel anxious. Sometimes these children will excel at assuming the worst, and this will drive their anxiety even further.

## Parental Habits

Your parents are most likely the most significant contributors to your adult anxiety, simply because they are usually the largest influencers in your life for the bulk of your childhood. Even well-meaning parents can fill their children with high anxiety levels to carry on into their adult lives. Despite their best intentions, some parents will inadvertently cause your adult anxiety, and sometimes it may seem that they did it on purpose.

You would not want to think that your parents were intentionally 'mean' to you when you were a child, but some parents seem to be aggressive to their children on purpose. If your parents, both or either one of them, used anger and aggression to motivate you as a child, then you might be carrying that in your adult anxiety. When parents punish more than they praise, they create children who might struggle with adversity later in life. While this might seem like just the opposite should happen, punitive parenting will cause a child to be overly critical of their own mistakes. When they carry this emotion into adulthood, they might be those who do not deal well with adversity because they have never really needed to face their failure. Their parents spent so much time guiding their activities that loss was not an option because it did not exist. So when these adults face adversity, they are unable to accept that they might fail at anything.

Children may also inadvertently pick up on their parents' anxiety and begin to internalize that anxiety. Parents who struggle to remain calm and in control will often raise children who have stress management problems. These children may be unable to cope with situations where they are facing doubt or uncertainty. They have no tolerance for stressful situations.

Parents who advocate too hard for their children will raise children who are unable to defend themselves. If the parents try to solve every one of their child's problems, they tell that child two things: the parent has no faith in the child's ability to take care of their issues, and the child can't come to the parent with little secrets. If parents dwell too much on their child's failures and not enough on their successes, they will raise children who focus more on the negative than the positive. For example, if the child gets a failing grade on a science paper, the parent immediately decides that the child needs help with science. Rather than helping the child, they reinforce the idea that failures are meant to be dwelt upon. On the flip side, parents who reside too much on their children's successes might raise children who are afraid to fail or have an overinflated sense of self. Suppose the child hits two home runs in one game, and the parent begins to image a pro career for the child. In that case, the child will either fear failing and disappointing their parents or believe that their abilities are better than they are, leading them to disappointment later in life when they don't succeed. The child may decide never to try anything new again because they can't live up to the parent's expectations.

Some parents spend their days so wrapped up in their standards and values that they cannot understand when their children have other beliefs. While it is essential to instill a sense of importance and integrity in children if they have a different set of beliefs and those beliefs are not harming anyone, they should be allowed. But many parents feel that their values are the only ones that matter, and if their children do not share their values, they must be rejecting the parents. And there are those parents who never let their children see them as anything less than perfect. While it is okay to protect children and shelter them from harm, there is nothing wrong with children seeing that parents will fail, they will have bad days, making poor decisions. If parents don't show this side to their children, they will never see how it is possible to make a mistake and recover from it.

## Siblings

Your siblings rank right below your parents for a source of anxiety since they are with you in your life almost as long as your parents are. From the moment they appear, or you appear according to the order of birth, you and your siblings are together. Many children grow up to have fantastic relationships with their adult siblings, but many more do not, and it is all because of behaviors that were learned in childhood.

Children will argue, and no one knows this better than a child who lives with their siblings. There will be quarrels in those houses with more than one child in the house. Most of them are minor and fade away as the children get older. But some will cause a lifetime of anxiety for the future adult. This phenomenon is particularly true if the adults in the family add fuel to the fire by acting out with the children. Sometimes parents will pit one child against another, and this behavior will add to the sibling rivalry.

Some sibling rivalry is normal because every child wants to be the best, most favorite child. It is when sibling rivalry erodes one child's self-esteem that the problems begin. Children who fight with their siblings about fairness and equality are more likely to develop anxiety issues that they will carry into adulthood. This inequality is not the standard, occasional conflict over who got the more significant piece of cake. This conflict is the issue that arises when one child always feels less wanted and appreciated because they perceive that their sibling still gets more than they do, whether it is time in the bathroom, freedom from chores, or the more significant piece of cake. And if a parent seems to be fostering this attitude and favoring one child over the other, then the child who feels left out will be confident that they do not matter.

When parents continually intervene in matters between their children, they rob their children of learning to work issues out with their peers and then move on. If the parents always take one child's side over the other in a conflict, then they are teaching the underdog that their opinion does not matter, that they do not matter. And if the parents pit one child against another, as they do when they compare the children to each other, they add to those feelings of anxiety. A child who is continuously compared unfavorably to a sibling will likely grow into an adult with terrible self-esteem issues. As adults, they are likely to defer their partner because they feel they don't matter anyway.

Commonly sibling aggression is dismissed as a regular part of growing up with other children in the house. But sometimes sibling rivalry will cross the line into bullying. If one of the children takes the role of bullying another child physically or verbally, and the parents are unaware or don't step in, the child who is the victim will be a victim. They will have feelings of anxiety that revolve around their worth in the partnership, and they will always feel that the other partner is in control. They may form an affiliation with an abusive person because that is the kind of relationship they know the best. Or they might create a relationship with a perfect person and be unable to fully commit to that relationship because they are afraid of being hurt again.

# Childhood Friends

We are naturally social creatures, and children are even more so. They want to have a best friend, want to be invited to parties and outings, and desire to be included as part of the group. Not all children will succeed in these goals, and some children will never be part of anything in their childhoods. Relationships with childhood peers are so meaningful for people to form the basis of adult relationships. Still, sometimes these childhood relationships are lacking in what the child needs.

Having a best friend or a few close friends is vital for everyone, but especially for children. Your best friend is the one you tell all of your secrets to, especially those you don't want your family to know. And you can tell your best friend about your childhood problems, and they will sympathize with you. They probably don't have the power to fix anything, but they will listen. And you will be there when your best friend needs you. Early learning is how a child learns the give-and-take of a relationship and how to get along on an intimate level with another person. Childhood friends will help each other put events into perspective. They will help to keep each other grounded and thinking naturally. Having a friend will help a child form the foundation of their future ability to cope with the world.

Some children do not have the chance to form intimate childhood relationships. They might be the child who is always outside the group, the child who lacks social skills. They might be the child who is constantly ridiculed for their physical appearance because in childhood being overweight, wearing glasses, having bad teeth, or bad hair, all of these are important. You need to look right so you will fit into the group. Sometimes children are not encouraged by their parents to make friends. Their parents may be overly protective and don't want their child around other children. The parents might need their child at home to perform household duties like babysitting younger siblings. Or the situation at home may be such that the child fears to make friends because they don't want anyone to know.

Childhood trauma causes adult anxiety. As an adult, those coping mechanisms that you learned as a child will still exist in your mind, no matter what your adult mind tries to tell you. Trauma is hard on people, especially children who don't possess the coping mechanisms an adult would have. Trauma will make a larger and more significant impression on a child. They will carry the pain and the after-effects of that trauma for many years, if not for the remainder of their lives.

Any sort of traumatic experiences like neglect, abuse, or abandonment, will need a coping response. Children have not yet developed the coping responses required to deal with adult issues because these issues are. They are adult problems that the adults involve their children with simply because they happen to live there. You might watch the neighbors fight and be strangely fascinated, but you are directly affected when the fighting is in your own home. Children cope in the only way they know how to at the time. They may become ill from internalizing all of that stress. They might try to overcompensate for their failings in preventing the conflict because, in a child's world, everything revolves around them, and they make everything happen, good and bad. The child might also simply disconnect from the experience and refuse to believe that it involves them.

If you experienced trauma as a child, whether it was an isolated event or an ongoing occurrence, you would carry the memory of that and how you coped with it into your adult life. You will bring learned helplessness into your adult life that will affect your adult relationships. It is how you learned to cope as a child, but it is not an accurate indicator of your real abilities. You are showing the helplessness you felt as a child in your adult situations. If you were helpless to stop your parents from fighting, you will probably not appease an angry partner unless you play the victim.

When you feel the anxiety, you might think you are trapped and that there is no way out of this mess. Panic and fear continue to cycle around you and through you, and you feel stuck in the situation. Because the anxiety you feel is so overwhelming, you might think you cannot break its hold on you. But if you can admit that you have a problem, you have taken that first crucial step toward getting rid of that problem.

Unlike adults who can walk away, the child has no choice but to suffer through the trauma. Adults possess the option to say how this anxiety will continue to affect you, especially in your relationships. There are methods for you to learn to accept your childhood traumas for what they were at that time, learn from them, and then put them in the past where they belong. When you decide to stop allowing your childhood traumas to rule your adult life, then you will be ready to rid yourself of your anxieties and move on with your adult relationships in a healthy manner.

# Chapter 4: Anxiety And You

There are so many articles that will detail the effect that your anxiety has on your physical, emotional, and mental health. That is all very true, and it bears paying attention to it because the constant stress of anxiety will negatively affect you. But people rarely talk about the effect that continual pressure will have on the health of their relationships. But anxiety can cause you to suffer from periods of tension, general uneasiness, feelings of overwhelming fear, and times of total panic. If you have overwhelming issues present in your relationship, there is a good chance that they are caused, at least in part, by anxiety.

## Your Anxieties

Anxiety can cause you to experience feelings of worry or fear, and these feelings might make you less aware of what your needs are in the relationship. These anxieties can also make you less aware of the needs of your partner in the connection. If all of your time is wasted worrying about things that might happen, it will be difficult for you to give appropriate attention to what is happening. When your anxiety is overwhelming, you then people around you might feel like you aren't really in the relationship, mentally and emotionally.

Procrastination and panic come from anxiety, squelching your authentic, inner voice. You might have trouble expressing the real feelings you are feeling and your internal needs. You may not be able to gain the amount of space or the attention you need because you cannot set reasonable boundaries. The boundaries that you need to develop are not always about keeping something out; sometimes, they pertain to things you need to have brought in. You try to postpone the experience of anxiety because it is not a pleasant emotion to feel. Or you might be driven by your fear to talk about issues immediately and endlessly when a small break from the problem might be the best thing for both parties. When you cannot say what you need and want, you will feel even more anxious. And you can become defensive and overwhelmed because your emotions may spiral out of control.

When you experience anxiety, you are experiencing an overactive response to fear. This response causes you to focus all of your attention on yourself and your problems. When this happens, your fears and worries can exude an unneeded pressure on your relationship. You feel that your anxiety is necessary to protect yourself and your best interests in the connection when your concern is keeping you from being vulnerable and compassionate with your partner.

If your partner shows signs of anxiety, you might react in selfish ways because you have built up resentments and fears.

Some fear and worry are perfectly normal in any relationship. That little tug at your heart that tells you things aren't quite right can put you on the path to getting to the root of a small problem and fixing it before it grows into a significant event. When you feel that everything in the relationship is continuously wrong, your anxiety is speaking. It will cause you to avoid the very things that might work to make your relationship better. You might feel like you are stuck in a particular situation if you are suffering from anxiety and never take the steps needed to improve your relationship issues.

Entering into any sort of relationship can often feel like you are playing some dangerous game with yourself. You risk being disappointed or even emotionally hurt when you seek companionship from other people. To begin and maintain a meaningful relationship will require you to display a certain amount of vulnerability. You may encounter a particular amount of anxiety by merely pursuing a relationship because of the relationship's unknown and uncertain outcomes. Untreated anxiety disorders can have a profound negative effect on your relationships with others. You may always worry about how other people judge you, so you might avoid dating or getting into a relationship to not be embarrassed or disappointed. If you struggle with fears of abandonment, you might worry that every future partner will eventually. You don't need to have an actual anxiety disorder to allow anxiety to ruin your love life. Any common daily fear can become worried about communicating with a partner, fear of going out on dates, or any generalized worry about the relationship process.

Relationship anxiety is widespread, and some of it is perfectly normal, even healthy for the relationship. There is usually some stress level at the beginning of a relationship since this is all new territory, and you are sailing in uncharted waters. No two relationships are exactly alike, and what worked in the last one might not work in this one. And even relationships of some duration can be hampered by relationship anxiety. The anxiety that you feel may not even be related to the relationship itself. Still, it will lead to behaviors that will create issues within your relationship. These anxieties can lead to physical complaints, emotional exhaustion, a lack of motivation, and complete emotional distress.

Relationship anxiety can make itself known in many different ways. Definitely in the early days of any relationship, there will be some insecurity about the relationship's progress. These anxieties usually pass quickly when you see that the other person is genuinely committed to making this relationship work. But there are also definite signs that you are experiencing relationship anxiety.

You might wonder if you even matter to the other person in the relationship. One of the most normal manifestations of anxiety in a relationship is wondering about your importance. This question brings up those underlying feelings of wondering if your partner will be there for you or if they have your best interests in their thoughts. This questioning shows a basic need for the partners to feel secure in their partnership. On a deep level, they need to connect with the other person and feel like they belong to something special. You may worry that your partner in the relationship is only there for the things you do for them. You might feel as though that person can't be trusted with serious matters, or you will question if they will miss you if you were gone.

You may begin to wonder if this relationship is really 'the one.' If you feel any anxieties about your relationship, you might continuously question your attachment to the other person. You may wonder if this is the partner for you or the connection for you. Even if the relationship is going well, you will question every aspect of it. You will wonder if this relationship is actually making you happy or if you just think it is making you happy. You may begin to focus on the little differences that point to your incompatibility.

You might spend all of your time wondering when they will break up with you. We always hope that all of the relationships we enter into will be happy, loving affairs. When the time is right, and the people are correct, the two people will feel satisfied, secure, and loved. You want to hold tightly to these feelings and hope they last forever. And in a good relationship, these feelings can last forever. But when anxiety creeps into a relationship, these good feelings will soon be replaced by persistent doubts and fears. You might worry that your partner is planning to leave you. Then you will make adjustments to your behavior to ensure that you will hold their continued affections. You will worry that they may become angry at you for some imagined event, even if they don't seem to be mad about anything. You will keep quiet when your partner does things that bother you instead of speaking up when you need something. And you will avoid discussing any issue that might cause a rift in the relationship.

You will begin to doubt that your partner has real feelings for you. Even when your friend makes sweet gestures and acts genuinely happy to see you, you may start to question every little thing that they do. In your mind, there is no chance that they like you. You will list ways in which you can tell that they don't really like you. If they do not always answer the phone immediately when you call or do not immediately respond when you text them, then they must be trying to avoid you. If they are not as open as you are, they don't feel the same way you do. If they are a bit distracted, then they must be thinking about ending the relationship with you.

When you have relationship anxieties, you will eventually end the relationship, either on purpose or by acting in a way that will drive the other person away. You might begin to test the boundaries of your relationship. You may keep telling your partner that nothing is wrong, even when something is, and they can know that it is. Some people will even start fights with their friends over insignificant matters. These are not things that you will intentionally do, but you will do them. And your goal, deliberately or unintentionally, is to test the strength of your friend or partner's feelings for you. Your subconscious tells you that you need to try them to see how much they care. But since this technique is all your doing, created in your mind, it is usually impossible for your partner to know what is going on.

Finding out what is causing the anxiety in your relationship will take some self-exploration measures and more than a little time. There is usually not one specific cause of the pressure that you are feeling. You may not even be aware of the real reason behind your anxiety. But your concerns reflect a fundamental longing for connection with another person in a meaningful way. The memories of the traumas you endured as a child will continue to affect your adult way of thinking, even if you think you are past them and have gotten over their effects. And the problems you face as an adult can add to the traumas from your childhood. You are more likely to experience relationship anxiety if a partner has ever lied to you about the depth of their feelings for you, not been entirely truthful about the kind of relationship they desire, unexpectedly left you, abused you in any way, or cheated on you.

When you have been hurt in any way, it is difficult to find the trust to put in someone new. Even if your current partner is entirely different from the one who hurt you, even if they never show any signs of dishonesty or manipulation, you might find it difficult to trust them and yourself. And your feelings of insecurity and doubt can be unlocked by specific triggers, even if you are not aware that these triggers exist.

If you are used to questioning everything, this may result in anxiety in your relationship. You may be one of those people who need to know the details about every situation. You might need to mentally explore all possible scenarios of a concern to determine how you will respond if certain things happen. You could be someone who carefully considers all angles of a problem before they make a decision. If you make a habit of always questioning your choices, even after you have made them and decided on a specific course, then you will likely spend a lot of your time asking about your relationship. This query is not always a problem because it is good to regularly examine some things to ensure that you pay attention to the things that need your attention. Significant decisions need your attention. But if you determine that you are frequently trapped in an endless cycle of indecision and questioning, you may have issues with anxiety.

The style of attachment that you develop in childhood will profoundly impact your adult relationships. Suppose you had caregivers or parents who quickly responded to your needs and supported and loved you unconditionally. In that case, your style of attachment is probably one based on security and safety. You don't worry about the support of the people around you because you trust that it will be made available when you need it. Your attachment style will be less secure if you were allowed to develop on your own or if your needs were not consistently met. There are different ways in which more insecure attachment styles can affect your romantic relationships. If you fear that your partner will suddenly leave you, then you have an anxious attachment. You love your partner, but you live in constant fear that they will leave you one day, and you will once again be alone. If you worry about deepening intimacy or creating a lasting relationship, then you are feeling avoidant attachment. You want to make an intense connection with this person, but you are afraid that if you do, you will not be loved the way you want to be loved, so you unconsciously push them away.

If you suffer from low self-esteem, this will spill over into your thoughts and feelings about any relationship. People who have lowered self-esteem will worry that they are making a good enough contribution to the relationship. If you are disappointed in yourself, then your friends and partners will undoubtedly be disappointed in you. If you feel that you are less desirable as a partner, your partner will find you less desirable. The failings that you see in yourself you project into the thoughts of your partner.

## Dating and Anxiety

If you are dating someone with relationship anxiety or being involved in a relationship with this person, you probably already understand how destructive these feelings can be. You might often feel like the anxiety is the third person in your relationship; the third wheel that makes being a couple just a little more complicated. This third person will get between you and your partner and sow confusion and doubt at every turn. You can't tell your heart where to love, and you certainly didn't enter this relationship with the idea that anxiety was going to fill your days with difficulties.

Anxiety does not need to ruin your relationship. It does not need to put such a strain on your relationship that you cannot enjoy being a couple or even make you think about calling it quits. If you understand how anxiety works and how it affects your relationship, you will be better prepared to overcome the effects of fear when it does enter your relationship. Overcoming the anxiety can push the two of you deeper into your relationship, making it healthier and more fulfilling than it was before. You need to be willing to accept the concept of relationship anxiety if you will help your partner and sustain your relationship.

- Anxiety is real, and it exists in your relationship. This anxiety is not something that your partner made up, and it is not something that you are imagining. It exists. Stress is every day, and it is only a problem if it threatens to overwhelm the relationship.
- The effects of relationship anxiety can prevent the two of you from enjoying the deep, meaningful relationship you were meant to enjoy.
- Anxiety is not necessarily life-threatening, but it can make your life miserable with dealing with it.

- No one wants to experience relationship anxiety. People who have this anxiety don't like it and don't want you to suffer from their problems.
- The symptoms of the anxieties can subside for long periods and then recur at odd moments. They may attack for weeks and months or only pop up occasionally.
- There is nothing rational or logical about anxiety. People who have concerns will fear things that don't exist and doubt things that may never happen. They will act irrationally at times. It will not help the situation. Tell your partner not to worry because this will probably make them worry more.
- Anxiety does not mean that you or your partner is weak. On the contrary, living with tensions and trying to hold together some normality in your life indicates you possess more inner strength than you think you have. It is not easy trying to live a good experience when the people who were supposed to help you as a child failed you and gave you all of these anxieties.

You need to be aware that a person who has anxieties does not look at the relationship in the same way. They will always be seeing things in a different light, imagining that things are other from how you see them. Your partner is probably spending a good part of their time worrying about the relationship and thinking of all the things that could be going wrong and probably already are. Having a few of these thoughts is sometimes familiar, and having many of them is not normal. When anxiety becomes part of your relationship, then your partner is probably thinking these thoughts all the time. Their mind is creating disastrous scenarios where the relationship goes sour, and they are left alone again. Sometimes their anxieties will make them act in ways that are guaranteed to annoy you or even push you away.

As an example, imagine that your partner is full of anxiety over the communication in your relationship. Your partner may feel that they are always the one to reach out first. They may question the length of time it takes you to respond to their phone texts or calls. They might feel that you would not even speak to them if they did not contact you first. So they begin to pull away and stop getting you. This strategy will force you to be the one to make the first contact if you want to talk to them. They may not answer the first few times immediately. They may be a test for you to see if you will continue to contact them even if you don't receive an answer in return. When they begin to feel better about your commitment's depth, they might become a bit more communicative. Knowing that you will contact them first makes them feel that they are worth the effort you are making. Their test was successful because you are still there. You have proven that their irrational fear that you are not as committed as they are is untrue. And this may only last for a little while before they feel the need to test you again.

## How Anxiety Destroys Relationships

Thinking that anxiety has the power to ruin a relationship might seem a bit dramatic, but it very well can. The pressure is an overpowering emotion that can cripple a relationship. When anxiety intrudes on one or both of the partners in a relationship, it will eventually creep on the relationship itself. Stress will affect your actions, emotions, and thoughts. It will lead to misinterpretations and cloud your perceptions and your judgment. Anxiety will drag you down into the pit of misery. When these things happen to one or both of the partners in a relationship, it has the power to cause them a considerable amount of misunderstanding and stress. The connection can be destroyed when anxiety is allowed to cause worries, make you wonder 'what if?', or taints your behaviors, thoughts, and emotions. These things will ultimately push out anything positive that once existed between the two partners.

When someone is living with anxiety, their life can become increasingly restricted as those anxious and negative beliefs and thoughts become the essential things in their lives. More relationship issues are experienced by people who have generalized anxiety. When anxiety intrudes into a relationship, the entire situation can become extremely stressful. Both the person who suffers from anxiety and their partner can suffer from the adverse effects of anxiety. The central theme in the relationship becomes stress. Greater distance comes between the partners as they begin to feel the barriers that the pressure causes them to erect. This division is an unhealthy situation that can easily lead to the death of the relationship.

The reason why anxiety has the power to ruin relationships is that it intrudes upon them. Stress not only causes people to have negative beliefs and patterns of thought, but it can also make those anxiety-ridden thoughts more massive than they are. The issues created by anxiety will erode the two partners' ability to trust each other and their feelings of being connected. The person who suffers from anxiety and their partner will spend too much time giving attention not to the relationship but to the stress itself. This misdirected attention will lead to feelings of abandonment, separation, and disconnection with each other.

If anxiety had its voice, it would use that voice to shout mean things at the partner of the person suffering from the tension and at the person who is suffering the anxiety. That is what fear does. It speaks with self-doubt words that will ultimately erode any rational thought either partner might have, and it will twist their stories into something unfriendly. The beliefs and opinions of the partner who has anxiety will cause them to feel negative emotions.

If the thoughts of anxiety would just stay as thoughts, they would be aggravating, but they would not have the power to ruin the relationship. But the concern is just not happy remaining as a thought; it must bleed over into behaviors and emotions. In relationships, certain kinds of anxious behaviors borne out of feelings and thoughts are quite common. These behaviors include avoiding honest and open conversations and displaying a host of negative emotions like punishing, rejecting, being cold, isolation, retreat, withdrawal, suspiciousness, possessiveness, jealousy, over-dependence, and clinginess. The overly anxious partner will need constant reassurance and will exhibit an extreme desire for physical closeness.

Living with the effects of anxiety can affect your relationship with your partner in various ways:

- Anxiety can destroy your ability to communicate effectively. Even if the other spouse is loving and supporting, the spouse who suffers from anxiety will often feel lonely. They may think that their partner does not truly understand their suffering and cannot fully explain their feelings.

- People who suffer from anxiety might act in specific ways that they might not normally behave. They may be 'acting out' to try to hide or erase their fears. They may take part in certain destructive behaviors like gambling, drinking, drug use, or cheating on their spouse.

- When one partner suffers from anxiety, the other partner might also be struggling with their own emotions. They may try to act in a way they think will make their anxious partner feel better emotionally when there is no way to do this.

- People struggling with anxiety might feel mostly unmotivated and uninspired by things they used to find joy in. These feelings will make it difficult for that person to find happiness in their hobbies, keep a job, or socialize. These behaviors can negatively affect the financial status of the couple or even social status.

- The partner who is struggling with anxiety might also struggle with intimacy. They will probably not be particularly interested in being intimate with their partner. Intimacy in a relationship will work to connect the souls and minds and the two partners' bodies. When intimacy is lacking or nonexistent, the entire relationship will suffer.

- People who struggle with feelings of anxiety are just generally unhappy. Anxiety will eventually shadow every part of your life and make you not even like yourself anymore. While you feel lonely, sad, and uninspired, your partner feels lost, scared, and helpless.

Anxiety will drain all of the life and love out of a relationship. You will be less aware of your real needs because your stress will cause you to worry or fear things that might happen. It will also make you less able to see what your partner needs. When you are worried about what might happen, you cannot pay attention to what is happening. And the overwhelming feeling of anxiety you are experiencing will make your partner feel as though you are ignoring them, which is a real possibility because you probably are and don't realize you are.

When you are feeling anxious, you will not be able to express your true inner feelings. And you might find it challenging to ask for either space or attention because you aren't really in touch with what you need. If you cannot express your true feelings, your anxiety will gradually become stronger until it overwhelms you. At those times, you may avoid the situation not to be forced to feel those uncomfortable feelings right now. At other times you might move a confrontation with your partner instead of waiting until you are calmer because your anxious inner voice tells you this must be decided right now.

You might spend too much time focusing on your problems or concerns when you are feeling anxious. Your partner may view your behavior as selfish because you are overreacting to your fears and concentrating on yourself. But your worries and concerns are putting unneeded pressure on your relationship because they will prevent you from being vulnerable and compassionate with your partner. These two things are vital to any good relationship.

Sometimes you might feel that something isn't quite right in your relationship. You might feel a tightening in your stomach or a short tug at your heart, those little inner signals that something might need to be addressed and fixed. But when your anxiety has built up to an unhealthy level, the feeling will be quite different. You might feel that your heart is permanently damaged or that you have a boulder sitting in your stomach. This feeling is because anxiety causes you to overreact emotionally and your body to overreact physically. You will avoid things that might make you feel better and something that would not harm you simply because you fear everything. Your anxiety will destroy your ability to make changes in your life that will make it better because you are terrified of doing anything different from what you already know. This fear of evolution applies to all situations. So you may have difficulty fully accepting your partner's love and affection because you fear what might happen if you allow yourself to be vulnerable. You may not be able to change your relationship, which may cause you harm because you fear the unknown.

Enjoying life and experiencing real joy means that you will need to feel free and safe in your relationship. If you have feelings of anxiety, then you might not ever feel those feelings of safety and freedom. Pressure causes feelings of worry and fear and robs you of any joy you might feel. The pleasure is depleted from your life because your anxiety renders you unable to experience your relationship's love and intimacy.

While anxiety will drive all of these behaviors, it is not just the person who suffers from the anxiety who will use these behaviors. And the reason that stress can ruin relationships is that the relationship can't possibly survive while these barriers to intimacy drive a wedge between the partners in the relationship. If the two partners are aware of how anxiety affects their relationship, they can save the relationship.

## Overcoming Anxiety in Your Relationships

The person who suffers from anxiety can suffer from excess tension, a general sense of uneasiness, feelings of overwhelming fear, and absolute panic. And all of these feelings will eventually overtake other parts of the person's life. The anxious person in the relationship is not the only one that suffers from the effects of anxiety. Your partner might want to help you, but at the same time, they might fear that your stress will bring them down. Worry will kill the love that might bring the two of you up together.

People like to think that the relationship's anxiety is the real problem, but the fear is only an outward indication of an underlying problem. Just like a fever alerts us to the presence of an infection, anxiety is the fever, and the underlying fear that causes the pressure is the infection. If you fear abandonment, you will either cling to your partner, fearing they will leave you, or you will be emotionally distant, refusing to allow yourself to be wounded again. Either of these emotions is not healthy for the relationship. But people like to think that anxiety is the problem because the fear will smother the love you feel, strangle the life out of it, and eventually tear it apart.

The one most important thing that you need to know about anxiety is that anxiety itself is not dangerous, and there is nothing wrong with anyone who feels fear. It is a normal human emotion, and it can be a powerful ally in your life. Anxiety is a fantastic tool; a sharp reminder that something is not quite right with this situation. It will help you to become more attuned to the little things that might have the potential to destroy your relationship. How you react to the anxiety you feel will determine whether your anxious feelings are harmful or helpful. Pressure will not be ignored forever; it wants you to acknowledge it, understand it, and act upon it. If you listen to your anxiety and consider a few truths about that anxiety, then you will be able to begin working on ridding your relationship of harmful stress.

There will always be some anxiety in a relationship. It is pervasive, especially if you are a person, who naturally worries excessively, or you or your partner has communication issues. Some anxiety will always be present in your relationship, and this might not be a negative thing. You are naturally drawn to love, the desire to feel connected to another person, and provide them with your love protection. You do this because you are a social creature who craves love and companionship. You will naturally feel anxiety if you don't feel connected to your partner. When you feel connected, you might still feel stress because you anticipate a future time when you will not be combined.

Feeling anxiety means that you care enough to worry about something. Your relationship might be the essential thing in your life, and you might fear that a time will come when it is gone. You value your relationship, and you care deeply about keeping it safe and well-protected. And if you feel that it is at risk, you will worry about it. You worry about your relationship, both working and not working. When you worry about your relationship, you will become confused, and you may not be able to hear the messages you need to hear. You will need to ask yourself if what you are feeling is protective anxiety in average amounts or if it is something more extensive and more profound. Your concern might be just about you, and it might be related to some stress in the relationship. You can begin to understand the source of your stress if you can be honest with yourself.

Everyone brings baggage into a relationship, those past personal experiences that made an impression on your emotions. This baggage is normal, and a very human reaction since your past experiences makes you the person you are today. The problem starts when those leftover fears from your childhood or past relationships cause your current relationship issues. If you are carrying baggage from a past relationship that you do not acknowledge and deal with, that baggage can cause flares of anxiety in your current relationship. The stress of this existing relationship that might be manageable will become unmanageable when mixed with the pressure of past relationships. This fear has the potential to make you quicker to react negatively to a situation. It can also make you less patient and more irritable. If you can see when your buttons are being pushed, you can change your feelings' focus if you can acknowledge when something makes you feel any anxiety. You will address the real problem before you and not focus your fears and concerns on the past issue that is clouding your current thinking. How you feel in your relationship, the time you spend with your partner, and your ability to communicate with your partner are all things that need your attention in the present.

You will need to ensure that pressures from external sources are not causing your relationship problems. Anxiety in a relationship can be caused by many external factors, such as pressures from society, religious affiliations, friends, and family. It is often difficult to separate the expectations we feel from other people and our sense of values. And you can not only absorb pressure from other sources on how to act in your relationship, but there might also be pressures about merely being in any relationship.

Suppose you spend more time fighting and less time communicating with your partner or feeling the strain of anxiety in your relationship. In that case, this is a good sign that the stress you are feeling is not the right kind of pressure. You may experience problems when the anxiety has been brought into the relationship or the relationship causing the stress. When the energy of the fear you feel is not channeled into a solution for solving the relationship problems, it will eat away at the relationship until the issue is either addressed or destroys the relationship.

Rather than ignore the anxiety in your relationship, a better approach would be recognizing what that anxiety is trying to tell you about your relationship. Try to see past the fear into what is causing it to channel your energy from the pressure into action. Maybe you are bothered by past issues trusting your partner, either this one or a previous one. Communication might be an issue if you feel that there is not enough communication or not enough of the right kind of communication. Always fighting with your partner about issues that are caused by anxiety but never really resolving these issues is unconstructive for the relationship. Having a bit of relationship anxiety is a good thing if it makes you do something to keep the relationship running smoothly. A small bit of pressure can make you want to improve yourself, the way you think and feel, the way you act and react, so that you can improve your relationship with your partner. Good anxiety will keep you focused on those critical things to you, those things that matter the most to you.

When you are stressed by the anxiety you feel, your defenses will be weakened, and you will then be more vulnerable to feeling the adverse effects of the fear you are experiencing. If an issue in your relationship leaves you feeling uneasy and feel good overall, you will have the energy to approach the problem and work with your partner to resolve it. The anxiety you feel will grow into an overwhelming feeling that will render you unable to work effectively with your partner to correct the problem if you are not in the right frame of mind or body. People in this situation will often take on self-destructive behaviors that will only mask the pain, not solve it. But temporarily, they will feel better and will be able to ignore the anxiety they are feeling. Now it will be a wrong time for you to overindulge in alcohol, food, or recreational drugs. It is also not the time to be careless with your health. You need to get the right amount of sleep, eat well, avoid alcohol and drugs, and just generally take more care of yourself. You will need the physical strength to be able to deal with the emotional issues.

Feeling confused and scared can be unsettling on a deep level, and feeling the effects of anxiety is no picnic. Feeling anxious might make you feel uncomfortable, but it is not necessarily a destructive emotion. The way that primarily determines how you are affected by anxiety and stress makes you feel. Fear does not play nice when it wants your attention. It wants you to make some sort of change. Rather than allowing your anxiety to evolve into something that you don't want it to be, try to keep the best possible perspective about the things that make you anxious and the fear itself. Relationship anxiety is perfectly normal even in the best relationships, especially if something in this relationship or past has given you a reason to worry. It does not need to be a valid reason, but it is your reason, and you need to own it. The most effective use of anxiety will be to improve your relationship, be more open and caring, learn to communicate more and more deeply. You should never be afraid to give a name to your anxiety because this will help you recognize it, and this is the first step in working through it. If you remember to think about your concern as something that can be useful and not something that is a problem in itself, you will use that anxiety to your advantage.

# Chapter 5: Overcoming Anxiety

Even though you may have experienced extreme trauma in childhood that dictates how you react to situations as an adult, you have the power to overcome the anxiety that threatens to cripple you and put it in the past where it belongs. You must go through specific steps to rid yourself of the demons writing the script for your adult life, but you will know true freedom for the first time when you do. Even if you do not totally rid yourself of your anxiety and only learn to accept it and work with it, you will then have the ability to enjoy your relationships the way they were meant to be enjoyed.

Anxiety is the type of problem that usually indicates the fear of a threat or some event going wrong in your future, as opposed to right now. Anxiety and fear are strong emotions that can last for a short time and then pass, or they might also last much longer, and you will feel stuck with them. They can even take over your life, affecting your ability to sleep, enjoy life, concentrate, eat, travel, or even leave the house or go to school or work. This anxiety can restrict you from doing things you want or need to do, and it also affects your health.

People are often overwhelmed by fear and desire to avoid those situations that might make them anxious or frightened. You may find it extremely difficult and upsetting to break this cycle, but it can be done in many different ways. You can adjust to feeling less fearful and better able to cope with fear to stop you from living. Lots of things make us feel afraid. Being afraid of some things – like thunderstorms or fires – can keep you safe. If you fear failing, that can make you try to do well so that you won't forget; it can also prevent you from doing something well if the feeling is too strong.

The things you are afraid of and how you act when you are fearful of something can vary from one person to another. Knowing what makes you afraid and why you are worried can be the first step to sorting out your problems with fear. Anxiety is an extreme form of fear, and the things you fear in your life are also valid reasons for concern. Stress tends to be used to express fear or when worry is nagging and persists over time. When you feel fearful about something in the future rather than what is happening right now, that is the feeling of anxiety. When describing the feeling of living with constant fear, most people will refer to that as anxiety. When you're frightened and anxious, the ways you feel are very similar, as the raw emotion is the same.

## Acknowledge Your Anxiety and Accept Its Influence

Many people will say that a particular event gives them anxiety when they feel nervous. You will feel uneasy when something is uncomfortable or unfamiliar, and this is perfectly normal. Feeling pressure and feeling nervous are two completely different things. Anxiety is characterized by excessive fear or worry. It has the power to affect your ability to go to school, hold down a job, or maintain a good relationship with that particular person.

Your first step will be to recognize that you have a problem with anxiety. People will often only seek help for the physical symptoms of anxiety, weight loss or gain, the inability to sleep well, and the headaches and stomach aches. They and their doctor don't connect their physical symptoms with the possibility of an emotional issue. And some people will deny that they have a problem with anxiety, or they may feel sensitive if the option is suggested to them. But the first step you will need to take is to admit that you struggle with the issues that anxiety brings to your life.

You will never be able to fix your issues until you can admit that you have them. Even though it feels more comfortable, your problems will not go away on their own just because you hope they will. You can forget your anxiety, and you can

85

pretend that it is not affecting your life. But your stress is affecting your life, and the sooner you can admit that the closer you will be to overcome it. Making excuses and denying the problem will not fix the problem. The initial step in fixing a problem is to admit that one exists because you can't fix something you don't know is there. As soon as you can acknowledge that you have a problem with anxiety, you can begin to figure out what causes your issues.

You might tell yourself that there is no way that you have a problem. But you do. You have difficulty maintaining a stable relationship with your partner because you let your anxieties from the past infringe on your current way of life. You desire a good relationship with your partner, but your concerns build walls that you can't quite get history. It will help if you get past yourself to get better because you are your own worst enemy in the case of anxiety. The defenses that you built in response to the traumas you suffered are now controlling how you arrange your adult life. The relief that these defenses give you will make you feel safe and reasonable, if only for a little while. Even if you are not self-medicating with substances like alcohol, drugs, or food, hiding behind the walls you have built, that is your way to protect your feelings from getting hurt again. You will continue to do anything in your power to feel that good feeling, even if it means destroying the very relationship you are trying to cultivate. All that matters is protecting you.

Now is the time that you need to do the exact opposite of what you feel like doing. You might feel like admitting that you have a problem with anxiety means that you are weak, but it means the exact opposite. Acknowledging that you have a problem with pressure proves that you dare to improve your life and relationships by learning to deal with your issues. Denying that you have a problem will cause you more harm in the long run. The longer you wait to address your anxieties, to harder they will be to overcome. Weak people will hide their problems and deny their existence. Strong people will admit that they have concerns and will want to do whatever is necessary to overcome those anxieties.

Do not avoid your anxieties because that will just make them worse. Admit to the things that make you feel anxious and realize that your stress will not be so bad the next time, now that you have accepted the fact that it exists. Prove your anxiety wrong because right now, it is running your life and ruining your life. Accept your feelings of anxiety for what they are and take the steps you need to take to overcome them.

## Know the Symptoms and Accept your Reactions

Your anxiety is usually driven by your anticipation of what might happen. It doesn't need to happen, and it may never happen, but it

en. Try not to give power to those
ocus your mind on where you are
id what you are doing right now. You
is though there is no past or future in
your life. Your anxiety level will begin to
decrease if you simply remain in the present.
Your anxiety level will increase if you allow
yourself to recall past failures, fear feeling hurt
or upset, or begin planning your escape from the
situation. Stay in the present.

When those first feelings of anxiety begin to
creep up, accept their presence. Do not attempt
to ignore them, control them, or fight them,
because right now, they are still in control of you
and the situation. Trying to get rid of them at
this point will only make them stronger in their
attempt to overwhelm you. See how your anxiety
fluctuates down and up, and try to give it a rating
for how strong it is. Slow down in your
acceptance if you feel that you are trying to do
too much too quickly. Allow yourself to feel
helpless or overwhelmed at times. Realize that
you can still handle this situation even if you are
feeling anxious. Continue doing those things you
need to do, even if you are feeling nervous about
it. You will not be wrong for not being in control
of the situation, as long as you do not feel totally
out of control.

Do not add to your anxiety with a secondary fear.
A secondary fear is the one that comes along
with your concern. You might feel that you will

be suddenly ill, faint, lose control, or do something embarrassing. These secondary fears often start with sudden thoughts that are tied to your anxiety. Your anxiety about opening your heart up to possible rejection has won again. The stress is every day, but adding to it is not normal. Feeling the secondary fear is normal, but you do not need to act on it. The same theory holds if you suffer from panic attacks when anxiety hits. Do not add secondary fear to the panic attack. Accept your concern and panic attacks for what they are and realize that they will pass on their own if you just wait patiently. Also, don't try to make the panic attack go away or try to fight it in any other way. It will pass.

Do not try to avoid or escape your anxiety. If you try to, you are just telling yourself that there is something wrong with you. Try never to make decisions based solely on what you are feeling but take a moment to consider all of your options. The memory that is causing you to fear is not the cause of your anxiety, but rather your imaginations of the horrible consequences that might happen. You will make a step forward every time that you accept your feelings and face your fears. Any time you try to avoid your feelings or escape your worries, you give up a remarkable ability to show the world that you are stronger than your anxiety. Maybe the situation that you are trying to avoid, the problem that fills you with dread is too large for you to correct all at once. There is nothing wrong with taking it in small doses. While you are doing it, try to remain calm. Tell yourself that you are perfectly capable of doing this and not feeling overwhelming anxiety. You must be willing to have the pressure, and you must be ready to fight your stress.

The goal here is not to make your anxiety go away forever but to change the relationship that you have with anxiety. You will need to be completely willing to feel your stress before you can make it go away. Try to make your reaction to pressure worse. Tell your palms to sweat more, your heart to pound harder, and your legs shake more. You probably can't do it, but you will see that your symptoms are beginning to subside in trying to do it. This lessening is because you have owned the feeling and shown it that you have the power to control it, and not the other way around.

You need to be committed to your recovery but not so rigid that you cause yourself even more anxiety. You do not need to be perfect. Anytime you are successful, no matter how small, give yourself some credit for your accomplishment. Never remind yourself of what you used to be like before anxiety took over because that person is gone forever. Sometimes you will not feel like you are accomplishing anything, and you will not feel any better than you did before. Show yourself some patience, and remember that these things take time. You did not become an anxious person overnight, and you will not be better overnight.

Never try to assume responsibility for those things that are outside of your control. Right now, you can't control the fact that you suffer from anxiety, but you can manage your reaction to those anxious feelings. So you are not responsible for having anxiety, but you are responsible for the way you react to it. Write your mantra, make it personal to your situation, and use it to tell yourself that everything will be just fine.

## Recognize your Anxiety and Learn to Cope with It

If anxiety is a part of regular life for you, you will need to develop strategies to keep it in check while overcoming it. There are things that you will need to do to begin on your path to wellness.

When your anxiety begins to flare, you need to take a moment to ask yourself to decide which past life event is making you feel anxious. You will usually feel anxious when a current event or feeling reminds you of a past event or feeling. No matter what matter you are worried about, one of the significant components of anxiety is that your feelings are not centered in the present. If you clear your mind of the past thoughts, then the pressure will begin to lose its grip on you. When your anxiety starts to move you out of the present, take a few minutes to regain control of your thoughts and emotions. Simply breathing deeply will help calm your feelings and give you a few minutes to regroup your thoughts. It will help to balance you and bring you back into the present.

Next, you will need to decide precisely what it is that is bothering you. You can quickly tell what your symptoms are, like your rapid heartbeat and trembling. It will not always be simple to determine what is causing those symptoms. But you will need to figure out what is bothering you if you want to get to the root of your anxiety issues. When you are not in the middle of an event, take some time to examine your thoughts and feelings about recent events. Whenever you have an anxious idea, try to take the time to write it down in a journal. You need to make a new habit where you work to reveal the causes of your anxiety because you will not be able to deal with them if you don't know what they are. And never be ashamed of your feelings. Feeling pressure is never anything to feel shame about because these feelings and reactions were given to you; you did not ask them. If you can uncover them and express them, you are one step closer to getting rid of them.

Sometimes anxiety will come from fears about an event that have not even happened yet and might not ever happen anywhere except in your mind. You might harbor fears about potential disasters, like the safety of those that you love, coming down with an illness, or losing your job or your relationship. You can't control life. What will happen in life will happen because life is an unpredictable thing. What you can do is to decide in advance how you will deal with those new things that cause you anxiety. Use all of the energy currently being used to feed your fear and anxiety and focus on developing future events' strength. Changing your attitude about your worries will help you to replace them with positive thoughts. If you are afraid that your partner will leave you, then ask yourself what would happen if they did. Plan your life in ways for how you would go on without them. This plan will accomplish two things. It will give you a project to follow if the awful something does happen, and it will make you recall how much you love your partner, which will provide you with a reason to face your problems and rid yourself of this anxiety. If you fear that something will happen to your loved ones when they are out of your sight, then try to spend as much quality time with them as possible. If you are afraid of losing your job, then remind yourself how lucky you are to have one, and always try to do your best work. It will take a bit of practice, but eventually, you will exchange your anxious thoughts with positive thoughts without even realizing that you are doing it.

Try to find something more pleasant to redirect your thoughts toward. This redirection is often the best course of action for you to take. There are many positive actions that you can take when your mind begins to run away with anxious thoughts. If your anxiety revolves around a memory from your childhood, try to replace that memory with a more pleasant one when the stress hits you. For example, if you are afraid that your partner will leave you because one of your parents left you and you fear abandonment, then replace the memory. Whenever you begin to think of your partner's anxious thoughts and remember your parent leaving, replace that childhood memory with happier times that you enjoyed with that parent. In good time, the anxiety will begin to subside, and you will be able to look at the childhood memory as what it is – an event that happened to the child you that you will not let affect the adult you.

# Chapter 6: Methods To Make You Calm

If anxiety is a part of regular life for you, you will need to develop strategies to keep it in check while overcoming it. There are things that you can do to begin on your path to wellness.

When your anxiety begins to flare, you need to take a moment to ask yourself what past life event is reappearing and making you feel anxious. You will usually feel anxious when a current event or feeling reminds you of a past event or feeling. No matter what issue you are worried about, one of the significant components of anxiety is that your feelings are not centered in the present. If you clear your mind of the past thoughts, then the tension will begin to lose its grip on you. When your anxiety starts to move you out of the present, just take a few minutes to gather control over your thoughts and emotions. Simply breathing deeply will help calm your feelings and give you a few minutes to regroup your thoughts. It will help to balance you and bring you back into the present.

Next, you will need to decide precisely what it is that is bothering you. You can quickly tell what your symptoms are, like your rapid heartbeat and trembling. It is not always apparent knowing what is causing those symptoms. But you will need to figure out what is bothering you if you want to get to the root of your anxiety issues. When you are not in the middle of an event, take some time to examine your thoughts and feelings about recent events. Whenever you have an anxious idea, try to take the time to write it down in a journal. You need to make a new habit where you work to reveal the causes of your anxiety because you will not be able to deal with them if you don't know what they are. And never be ashamed of your feelings. Stress is nothing to feel ashamed of because these feelings and reactions were given to you; you did not ask for them. If you can uncover them and express them, you are one step closer to getting rid of them.

Sometimes anxiety will come from fears about events that have not even happened yet and might not ever happen anywhere except in your mind. You might harbor fears about potential disasters, like the safety of those that you love, coming down with an illness, or losing your job or your relationship. You can't control life. Life is unpredictable and life will happen. What you can do is to decide in advance how you will deal with those new things that cause you anxiety. Use all of the energy currently being used to feed your fear and anxiety and focus on developing future events' strength. Changing your attitude about your worries will help you to replace them with positive thoughts. If you experience fear of something in particular happening, then ask yourself what would happen if it did. Develop a plan outlining how you will react to the situation. This plan will accomplish two things. It will give you an idea to follow if the awful thing does happen, and you will reaffirm your strength and ability to face this anxiety. If you fear that something will happen to your loved ones when they are out of your sight, then try to spend as much quality time with them as possible. If you are afraid of losing your job, then remind yourself how lucky you are to have one, and always try to do your best work. It needs a bit of practice, but eventually, you will exchange your anxious thoughts with positive thoughts without even realizing that you are doing it.

There are effective ways to address your anxiety so that you can learn to live a calm life. Some of these techniques will help you when you are feeling anxious, and some of them will help you change your life in meaningful ways so you will feel more in control of your life. Use several techniques together for the best effects.

## Visualization

This is a powerful tool that will allow you to relax and get rid of stress. It uses images in your mind to put you into a more relaxed state. Visualizing is somewhat like daydreaming because visualization is accomplished by you making use of your imagination.

Visualization will help you cope with anxiety in several ways and help you work with stress and other disorders related to anxiety. Think about how your feelings and thoughts are so disordered when you suffer from panic or anxiety. Your mind will probably focus on the worry when you are in the middle of a panic attack. Your fear will grow the more you focus on thoughts of what might happen. You will learn to push aside your fears when you visualize happier thoughts. You will focus on calm and serene images to fight your fears.

You will need a comfortable environment to maximize the benefits of visualizing. Eliminate any possible distraction so you can completely relax. Select a place that is quiet where you will be less likely to be disturbed. Wear comfortable clothing and remove your jewelry. Assume a comfortable position by either sitting in a comfy chair or lying down somewhere in a comfortable place.

First, it can help slow your breath by doing some deep breathing exercised for a few minutes. Shut your eyes and release any tension you may be experiencing anywhere throughout your body. You may need to try a muscle technique for progressive relaxation before beginning your visualization to relax even further. Set aside a specific amount of time to visualize.

Picture in your mind a white sandy beach where you are relaxing and feeling safe. Relax deeply as you think about the following:

- The sun shining warmly on your body
- The soft lapping sounds the waves make
- Sinking comfortably into your oversized beach chair
- The soft white sand warming the bottom of your feet
- The perfect temperature aided by the massive umbrella standing near enough to provide you with some shade

Let your face relax as you release all of the tension in your forehead, relax your face around your eyebrows, soften your neck, and loosen your throat. Slow your breathing to the tempo of the rolling waves in the water. You are not putting out any effort to be here; spend your time relaxing soaking it all in. When your relaxation is complete, imagine yourself getting up and walking slowly and deliberately back from the water. You can return to this beautiful place anytime you need to come back. Slowly open your eyes and relax a bit before you move.

If going to the beach does not quite fit your style, then put together your own visualization. Think of someplace that you have always found to be very enticing. You might see yourself strolling through wide open fields, or you might be seeing a beautiful vision from the top of the mountain or deep in the forest. When you visualize your own version of a calming scene, you will want to experience the scene by using all of your senses. See how the experience makes you feel in your body and spirit. Do not leave your place until you feel ready to go, take your time while you are there, and gradually allow your thoughts to return to the present.

The more times in a day that you can practice visualization, the faster you will improve at the practice. Techniques for relaxation are generally more beneficial if you first start using them when you are calm and not anxious. Using regular practice, you will more readily turn to visualization when it is really needed, like in those times when you are feeling the onset of panic and fear as physical symptoms.

## Physical Exercise

Maintaining mental fitness is vital, and regular exercise can assist with this along with relieving stress. Function will improve and fatigue will reduce when you exercise. This enhancement is definitely beneficial when your stores of energy have been depleted by stress or you have lost the ability for concentration.

When stress negatively affects your brain, with its numerous connections of nerves, the remainder of your body will feel the effect. Your brain will function better when your body feels better. The painkiller hormones called endorphins are released by your brain when your body engages in exercise. They lower your stress and help you sleep better.

Those people who are already mentally healthy swear by the beneficial effects of exercise. Increasing daily physical activity is known to improve your levels of energy, enhance mood, and promote better quality of function.

Physical exertion is good for your mind for many reasons:

- Exercise decreases the levels of stress hormones. Activity will lower the stress hormones such as cortisol. Endorphins will increase those hormones that give your mood a natural boost.
- Physical activity takes your conscious thoughts away from your feelings and thoughts that are negative. It can redirect your mind away from your current problems and work to turn it to the activity at hand, like the physical exertion or send you into a state of Zen.
- Exercise develops physical and mental confidence. It will help you lower your weight, tone your body, strengthen your muscles, and achieve and hold onto your natural beauty. You might begin to feel a definite sense of elevation in your mood.

Your aura will glow and your clothes will compliment your body.

- Exercise will provide you with a definite source of support from society. Social support benefits are desirable when you are suffering from anxiety, and many practices are natural public activities as well. You can join a class for exercise, or join a league to play sport. As long as you are exercising with others, you will enjoy relief from stress in more than one way.

- When you improve your physical health, the health of your mind will also improve. Stress can make you feel sick, and feeling ill can cause you to handle stress. Using physical exertion to improve your physical and mental health will relieve much of the tension in your body. This exercise will keep you feeling healthier, both physically and mentally, which will also keep you feeling healthier.

- Physical activity will remove most of the stress from your body, and it will provide you with the strength to cope with the stress in your life. People who engage regularly in physical activity feel less stress in other areas of their lives.

Walking is a marvelous way to reduce the effects of anxiety and help you remain calm. The part of your brain that controls pressure is one of the oldest and most primitive parts of your mind. This is the reason why making decisions when you're anxious is almost impossible, and making too many decisions can make you nervous. This nervous part of your brain is straightforward can do only one thing at a time. Walking will shut down the anxious mechanism in your mind, so while you are walking, the nervous part of your brain can shut off a bit. Walking will give you distractions for your senses to enjoy. When you are walking, you can process the information you are gathering from around you. Even walking around inside you in your house will help use your brain to process new items.

A practical method for dealing with anxiety is merely reducing the amount of time you spend thinking about it. You will only elevate your stress if you spend too much time thinking about it. You will make it difficult for your brain to focus on your anxiety by simultaneously making it process several different information types. Your mind needs the distraction from other sensory outlets and the stimulation that comes from healthy sources such as nature. This stimulation will also help defeat your symptoms. Walking in nature has extra benefits. Trees and plants emit beneficial chemicals that can calm your mind and significantly impact your anxiety levels.

Another way to increase your walk's effectiveness is to go to expansive places that give you a sense of awe. Your oxytocin levels increase when you are in comprehensive places, those places that make us go stop and stare, entranced in the breathtaking view. Oxytocin is the hormone that is released here, making you feel relaxed and calm.

## Meditation

Anxiety is your body's way of saying there is too much stress going on.  This feeling happens to everyone. But, when you feel that you are always on alert and it becomes the background noise to your life that will not go away, that is when you need to seek help. Mindfulness and meditation practices for anxiety relief are growing fields that can help you navigate the many ways that fear can disorder your life. Here is one method you can turn to as you begin to lower the anxiety levels in your life.

It is possible to calm your anxiety in three simple steps. Begin by opening your attention to the present moment. The invitation is to bring attention to your experience more broadly and openly that isn't involved with selecting or evaluating. You want to simply hold still mentally and become a container for thoughts, feelings, or sensations in your body that are present.  See if you can watch them change from one moment to the next. Focus on your breath. Let go of that comprehensive view of events and bring your focus into a more concentrated and centered view. Bring your attention to your body. Move your awareness out to become aware of sensations in your body as a whole. Sit with your whole body, your full breath, and then once again move back to a broader and more spacious view of attention for your experience.

Mindfulness is not the best choice for everyone. But when you can create a little space between yourself and what you are experiencing, your anxiety can soften. If you become too accustomed to that low rumble of stress always being there, it will gradually grow, creating a habit of stress and anxiety that will undermine your health and well-being. Consequently, when you become caught up in reactivity patterns, we make more distress in our lives. This distress is why it is essential to clearly understand the difference between reacting with unawareness and responding with mindfulness.

Mindfulness helps you learn to recognize your complicated feelings without needing to analyze, suppress, or encourage them. Allowing you to feel and acknowledge your irritations, painful memories, worries, and other complicated feelings and thoughts will often help them dissipate. Mindfulness will enable you to spend valuable time exploring the causes that underlie your stress and your anxiety safely. Going with what is happening right now in your life instead of trying to run away from it or fight it, you create an opportunity for your mind to gain knowledge into what is elevating your worries. Mindfulness allows you to build space around your worries, so they will not consume you. When you spend time understanding the underlying causes of your fears, you will come out on the other side with a sense of spaciousness and freedom.

Mindfulness is the essential desire to be present fully, only knowing the events that are happening right now, and not becoming overly reactive or overwhelmed by what is going on around you. When you hold your awareness in the present moment, you gain access to inner reserves of strength you may not have realized with you all along. You will find stillness in your core, along with an awareness of what you need and don't need in your life that is with you all the time. Practicing mindfulness might not change your situation, but it will allow you to change your response to your problem. Here is a meditation script you can use when you feel stressed or use it daily to keep yourself calm and relaxed.

Focus on your breath first. The key to being relaxed is breathing calmly. Inhale deeply into your nose. Then exhale fully out through your mouth, the way you would if you were puffing out a candle. Push all of the air out. When you breathe in, set your focus to slow down your breath into a slow rhythm that is calming. Release all of your air you took in when you exhale. Keep up the breathing in and out. Now as your body is bringing in the oxygen that it needs, the only other task now to concern you is to remain as calm and steady as you can until the feeling goes away. Your anxiety will become heavier when you fight it, so at this moment, accept the idea that you are now feeling anxious. Focus on relieving your stress by calming your thoughts. Repeat this following phrase:

*I have anxiety at this time, but I still feel okay. These feelings always go away, and I will not be harmed by waiting a few minutes. While I may feel frightened, I know I am perfectly safe. I will feel peaceful again soon, even though right now I am feeling anxiety. This feeling will pass, and I will survive. I will stay as comfortable as I can while waiting for the pressure to go away. While I wait for the feeling to go away I will keep myself relaxed and calm.*

Continue to breathe slowly and mindfully in and out. Now you can work on any physical feelings you are having as you continue to repeat calming thoughts. Your body jumps into fight-or-flight mode when you experience anxiety. Your body delivers oxygen to your muscles as your heart beats faster to provide the power for you to enable those muscles to run away from danger. You are in no real trouble at this moment, so while the feelings of fear are flowing in your body, it is not being utilized. Your large muscles are trembling because they are so ready for action.

You can physically shake out the tension to help this trembling to decrease. Pretend that you are drying your hands by shaking the water off. You just washed your hands, and there is no towel available. Small children do this all the time, even if a towel is single. Shake your hands gently in midair. Keep your arms and hands slightly soft as you wiggle your forearms and hands front and back rapidly. Imagine little droplets of water flipping off of your fingertips. Picture your stress flowing out of your fingertips and gradually being shaken all away. Now cease shaking and let your hands hang still. Your hands will feel much more relaxed and pleasantly tingly.

The final area for you to focus on to get rid of anxiety is the tension in your muscles. They become tired, sore, and stressed when you are feeling stress or anxious. Now you will relax your muscles by first dropping the lower half of your mouth open, so your teeth are not touching. Relax your jaw and let your mouth be loose. Then drop your shoulders slightly. Let the shoulders be open and flexible. Gently circle your shoulders and arms in small circles, backward and forward, and then allow your shoulders drop even more to make bigger the space between your head and shoulders. Stretch your arms up over your head and then let go of the muscles as you slowly lower the arms back down to your sides. Tilt your head slowly to look to both sides a few times. Keep your head softly relaxed. Bring your spine back to a straight posture. Make your spine straight with the natural curving of your back. You will release more tension as you keep on moving, stretching, and relaxing, and this will let your muscles to not be quite so tense.

## Yoga

Stress will negatively impact your life in so many different ways. Your symptoms of stress will definitely affect your body and your health. The majority of the causes of anxiety are usually accompanied by physical and emotional symptoms that are negative and cause distress. It is often difficult to manage these thoughts and feelings, and dealing with them can lower your quality of life. All of the recommended techniques for relaxation are found in yoga. It will also reduce your stress, reduce the feelings of nervousness, and increase your practice of mindfulness. There are many reasons why yoga is recommended for anyone who suffers from anxiety.

Yoga will revitalize and renew your body by elevating your strength, increasing your sense of balance, and extending your flexibility. An authentic lifestyle that surrounds yoga will include a practice that goes far beyond simply exercising physically. The exercises for breathing and meditation are part of yoga practice, which will help calm your mind and release your stress. Practicing yoga can also help manage fears, panic, and anxiety, given the many stress-reduction benefits. Anxiety and panic bring many uncomfortable symptoms, like the feelings of tightness, tension, and elevated sensitivity to pain. The postures of yoga, the asanas, will lessen the physical discomfort building in your body caused by anxiety. Postures work on stretching, lengthening, and balancing the muscles. These poses will help release the tension building up in your muscles and ease the stiffness that is built up throughout your body.

The poses work together in ordered sequences that are a powerful way to do physical exercise. Exercise is well known to reduce symptoms, including lowering the effects of pain and stress. Yoga relieves anxious thoughts while it relieves physical aches and pains. Patterns of thinking negatively and worrying frequently are normal for anyone dealing with anxiety. Using all of the tools available to you can help you avoid fear and panic. The general yoga practice will bring out the response of relaxation, letting both your mind and body to gather a feeling of calm and ease.

Yoga will also give you an excuse to get out meeting other people. You can exercise while feeling more connected to other people with a sense of belonging. Often people who have anxiety and agoraphobia also face loneliness and isolation because they may fear being around other people. When you take part in a yoga class, you can begin to socialize with others while you all work toward personal wellness.

Use the Standing Forward Bend anytime you feel stress building, and you need to alleviate it to remain calm. This pose can be done anywhere because it does not require a mat. This position is a very beneficial pose that can be used at any time. Do this anytime you feel the need and before you engage in anything that may create anxiety. It will provide you with energy while letting go of tension.

Stand tall with your feet near each other. Keep your straightened spine long as you lift your arms up and then bend forward, lowering from your hips when you fold your body in half while still facing forward, reaching your hands down to touch your toes. Hang there limp and loose and hold your elbows softly with your hands. Allow the heavy feeling to release from the upper half of your back, shoulders, and your head, which are the areas in which you usually hold onto most of your stiffness. Leave your eyes closed and suck in deep and steady breaths, letting your thoughts go away.

Tree Pose is another pose that will help relieve anxiety and bring you to a state of calm. Tree pose is fundamental in easing stress. By using essential balance while standing, you will create concentration and awareness, to take your mind off of the stress and focus on your physical health.

Standing up straight and tall with your feet slightly apart, shift most of your heaviness to your right side leg. Bend your left side knee outward, and put the flat bottom of your left side foot onto your right inner part of your thigh or right below your knee, keeping your toes pointed down to the floor. Keep your pelvis centered directly over your right foot. Press your left foot's sole into the flesh of your inner right side thigh while pushing back with your outer right side thigh. Press your hands together before you with the palms together. You can gaze toward the ceiling or straight forward. Hold still for three to five seconds, and then repeat the sequence on the other side.

## Self-Hypnosis

Unlike what has been portrayed in popular culture, you do not lose complete control while under hypnosis. You will not be brainwashed and your mind will not be taken over.

Instead, the true practice of hypnosis is to reach a state of peace and focus that is elevated. You will communicate directly with your subconscious by shutting down your conscious mind. That part of your mind is extremely open to receiving new ideas and suggestions when you are in this state. Hypnosis can be thought of as meditation that has a particular goal. That is because in both you will look for a similar frame of mind.

The difference you will find is that with hypnosis, you are not just relaxing your mind. You want to work directly with your subconscious. You can provide it with vital new information and different methods for processing the information it gets from the outside world. You will utilize repetition so you can start to reprogram your subconscious mind to come out in methods that are more helpful. When you utilize self-hypnosis, you will practice by yourself in the privacy of your own home.

You will complete all of the steps that are recommended to attain hypnosis. But you will be completing it by reading from a script for hypnosis. You can use self-hypnosis almost anywhere. It is particularly useful before any experience that might be stressful or to help you respond to a situation when you might feel anxious. Self-hypnosis is something you can work on every day if you want. You can also do self-hypnosis anywhere that you are that you do not need to be alert and focused. Master this method, and you can use it throughout your life.

Self-hypnosis begins with relaxing your body and mind. The most common method used for this step is deep breathing. Therefore, you might need to breathe deeply a few times before you start. You prepare your body when you begin with relaxation so it will be able to let go of worry and enter that peaceful place of mind.

Self-hypnosis works with a script you will follow to make your mind relax. Most scripts you will find will walk you along through the process so you will attain the state for hypnosis. The process might start out with something as necessary as doing a countdown or reciting some affirmations for positivity. You will enter a hypnosis state when your mind and body are relaxed, and this state is similar to daydreaming.

When you are in the state of intense peace and relaxation, you will gain access to your subconscious and talk to it directly. Now your subconscious will be very open to your suggestions, and this is what the hypnotic affirmation is. It is an idea or suggestion that is related to anxiety and is worded in a positive manner. These suggestions form the basis of hypnosis by allowing you to release the subconscious feelings that already exist and that keep you stuck in one place.

Many of the scripts will include periods of visualization. You might need to visualize yourself as someone free from worry. Picture yourself as a well-collected person who is full of confidence. This visualization helps to reinforce your suggestions. You will learn that you will prefer to keep yourself in this state of relaxation

114

until you are fully ready to awaken yourself and go on about your day.

One great thing about hypnosis is that you will process results after your very first session. These early results might be quiet, or they can be relatively intense. But letting your mind fully unwind and your body completely relax will undoubtedly provide you with some relief from your anxiety. Benefits from hypnosis that you will experience include:

- Hypnosis provides you a sense of mental clarity so you will feel refreshed afterward.
- After a session of hypnosis, your symptoms of stress will most likely have decreased. Practice some self-hypnosis before you attend a social situation that is stressful. Your confidence will increase and your stress decrease.
- Anxiety will increase your stress and make your thoughts. A session with self-hypnosis will work to help you to elevate your moods in a matter of a few minutes.

It will take time to achieve long-term results. Self-hypnosis is a skill that will require vigilance and practice. Do not expect to immediately attain the exact same state as another person who has been practicing for several years. With regular practice, the self-hypnosis will become easy to attain. You will probably experience a lowering in your symptoms or a calming sense of clearness that will follow your first session of self-hypnosis. Lasting benefits can occur after just a few sessions.

Here is a sample script for self-hypnosis that you can use at any time you can relax and be calm. It is not recommended for those times when you need to be alert. Record yourself reading this calmly and then play it back whenever you feel the need to relax. Get into a comfortable position somewhere that you can relax completely. If it helps you feel more relaxed, put on comfy clothes, and use a soft blanket and pillow. The idea with self-hypnosis is to relax and be comfortable and learn how to be calm.

*Now you will use your imagination for a little while. Picture yourself standing in a beautiful meadow full of flowers of all sizes and shapes. Picture all of the beautiful colors in your mind's eye. Smell all of the unique scents that are filling your nose and overpowering your sense of smell. Breathe deeply in and out so that you can fill all of your reasons with the beautiful aroma of the many flowers that you see before you. As you breathe deeply in and out, listen to the birds' sounds, calling out to one another among the flowers. Listen to their beautiful birdsong as they swoop and dive, playing among the gorgeous colors and scents. The sun is warm as it shines brightly on you, warming your face with its rays. Lift your hands to the sky and feel the warmth of the sun warming your hands, making them soft and relaxed. The sun is perfect in the sky; it is just right as it shines warmly on you.*

*There is a flat space of grass in the middle of the flowers that you can see ahead of you. Lying on the soft grass is a fat pillow and a large, soft blanket. You want to lie down on this soft blanket and relax in the warmth of the sun. Lie down, and feel yourself begin to relax even further. Lay your head on the pillow. It is wonderfully soft and completely cradles your head as it caresses you with its softness. You knew it would be this wonderful. You could see it. Lie on your back on the blanket and stare up into the cloudless blue sky. While you are staring, you realize that your eyelids are growing heavier and heavier. Close them and feel the warmth of the sun on your face. Your legs and arms are heavy and limp as you lie on the blanket under the warm sun. You are now completely relaxed and calm, lying on the mantle in the warm sun.*

*Now keep your eyes closed and use only your mind to see things. Picture yourself strolling toward a flight of stairs. You have no fear of the stairs. You have relaxed completely, and you are safe and secure. Look at the stairs for a few moments. See the railing leading down, a safe thing for you to hold on to. See how complete and sturdy the steps themselves are, to keep you*

*safe as you walk down them. Lay your hand
lightly on the handrail as you stand at the top of
the staircase. I will begin to count backward
from ten, and when I start, I want you to start
walking down the steps, one stair at a time.*

*As you walk down the stairs, you will feel more
relaxed with each number's passing than you
did on the stair before. Now set your hand on
the railing, the safe and secure bar, and when I
say ten, you will step down the first step. Ten:
go ahead and step down. You are relaxed as you
begin to take your actions. The stairs are sturdy
and safe, and the railing will keep you from
falling. Nine: step down and feel your body and
mind relax even more. Eight: you have now
gone down two steps. Feel how your body is
sinking further into a state of relaxation. Seven,
six, five: you are now halfway down the stairs,
and everything is okay. Your mind and body are
well relaxed, and you have no cares. Four: feel
how the banister slides smoothly under your
hand, and the steps support you sturdily. Three:
you are almost to the bottom of the staircase.
Two: you are now so relaxed and calm that you
could easily fall into a deep sleep. One: you are
at the bottom now and peaceful and serene.*

*Now that you are at the bottom of the stairs,
you can see the large piece of white paper
hanging on the wall. Walk toward the sheet of
paper. See the table underneath that is holding
all of the markers in a rainbow of bright colors,*

*any color that you might imagine. Choose whichever color that you like the best and pick up that marker. Now you will use the marker to draw a square on the board. Make the square about twelve inches or so on each side. When you have drawn the square put the marker back down on the table; now pick another color that you find pleasing and pick up that marker. Use it to draw a circle inside of the square. Ensure the lines of the ring touch the lines of the square wherever possible but do not go outside of the square. Then put that marker back on the table.*

*Now pick up a third color that you like and use that marker to draw a triangle inside of the circle. The triangle points should touch the lines of the circle but should not go outside of it. Now put that marker down and choose another one that you will use to draw a square inside the triangle, letting the square's points touch the triangle's lines. Now select another color to draw a circle inside the square, just barely allowing the circle's lines to connect the square. Keep this marker in your hand as you step back and admire your picture for just a moment. Now take this same marker and use it to fill in the circle. Fill the circle in thoroughly, making sure that no white space is leftover that anyone might see. Now take the black marker off the table and put a black dot centered in the circle. Directly stare at that black dot, stare with all your powers of concentration, your body relaxed, your limbs limp and relaxed, staring at the black dot. Feel the wind begin to suck through the black spot from where you are standing. See the black dot expand slightly as you feel the power of the wind blowing through it. Relax completely while the power of the wind rushing through the black dot pulls you headfirst through the bubble. Your body, completely relaxed and limp, quickly passes through the black dot with the force of the wind until you find your entire body on the other side of the wall in a room just big enough for you.*

*No one knows you are in this room. No harm can come to you in this room. This room is your safe space where you will go to relax and be calm and escape from your anxiety. When you begin to feel anxious, just come down the stairs slowly and draw the paper's shapes. Create the black dot in the middle and let the power of the wind pull you through the bubble and into your safe room. Nothing will find you here. Nothing can get to you here. There is no fear or anxiety. There is only peace and calm in this serene, tranquil place. Come here when you feel fear or when you feel stress creeping up on you. Relax long as you need to, keeping your mind and body calm and relaxed. You are flexible. You are peaceful. You are serene and tranquil. You are safe and secure. You have no worries or fears. You are safe. You are safe.*

# Herbal Remedies for Calm

Anxiety originates in your brain in an area that regulates your body's response to stress. When you perceive danger, your body's stress response sounds the alarm and releases a torrent of hormones, including adrenaline and cortisol. This hormone prepares your body for your reply. This natural trait is key to your survival. But when your alarm gets stuck in the open position, and the hormones never stop flooding your body, then hypervigilance turns into anxiety. For some people, it feels like a racing heart or a queasy stomach. In others, it creeps in like a fog of overwhelming emotions or a persistent sense of dread.

Using plants to overcome anxiety is less mystical than it may sound. Herbs enhance the calming influence on your mind. Always take necessary precautions when using any treatment, and this includes herbal remedies. Always follow the directions on the packaging. Some herbs will interact poorly with other medications, which is another reason to do your homework first. Begin with the smallest possible dose recommended for adults and see how it goes. And, of course, if you are on prescription drugs, check with your healthcare provider before layering on an herbal antianxiety.

Chamomile is an ancient and widely used medicinal herb. Chamomile has many calming elements. It is typically used for mild anxiety. You can use this herb in many forms, but herbal tea is the traditional form used to ease stress. Pour hot water over two to three heaping teaspoons of dried chamomile, steep for five to 10 minutes, then strain. Drink as needed throughout the day.

Ashwagandha helps the body rein in a runaway stress response by addressing chronically high cortisol and adrenaline. Over time, ashwagandha helps lower the stress response in the body back to normal levels. It may immensely benefit anxiety sufferers with a history of trauma, who often experience anxious hypervigilance. Take ashwagandha for at least three months.

Kava is perhaps the best-known herb for anxiety relief. This herb acts quickly, usually in less than twenty minutes. This speed makes it useful in acute situations where stress relief is needed immediately, like after nearly having an accident, an angry conversation, or anytime your stress response activates. The best benefit is that kava relaxes your muscles without sedating your brain. Muscle tension can enhance, exacerbate, and amplify your feelings of anxiety. When anxiety strikes, take a few drops of kava tincture in a small glass of water. Your lips may tingle a bit.

Rhodiola supports mental focus and functions related to memory. It is also used to treat immune depletion resulting from radiation, chemotherapy, overwork, and other stressors. It quickly assists with stress, especially for stressful tasks like studying for an exam or rushing to meet deadlines.  Rhodiola is suitable for supporting and restoring a strained-adrenal system.  Rhodiola might be mildly stimulating to some people, so it is best taken in the morning or early afternoon. This herb is available in many forms, and all are useful.

Passionflower can relieve anxiety-induced insomnia. The herb's flavonoids and alkaloids interact gently silence the body's alarm bells. Most people find this herb to be both mentally and physically relaxing. Besides relaxing you for enhanced sleep, passionflower can help calm that part of your mind that anticipates fears. Nighttime waking is a common sleep complaint among people with anxiety. Keep a glass of water with a few drops of passionflower extract on your bed table.

Lemon balm relaxes your body without sacrificing the clarity of your thinking. Lemon balm is the best choice for quickly cooling off the sympathetic nervous system. Although this herb is usually combined with other herbs for calming and sedating, such as lavender, valerian, and hops, it is best to try it on its own first.

**Making herbal teas** – the beauty of herbal teas is that you can use herbs to keep you calm along with herbs that you like to drink, and you can drink tea all day long, every day. Teas made from herbs are delicious, either hot or cold. So in the morning, prepare a glass of herbal tea and take it with you to start your day off right. You can purchase herbs to make tea blends but try to buy them from dealers who do not add extra flavorings or chemicals. If you feel even more motivated, you can try growing your herbs for your herbal tea.

Herbal teas are made with a particular structure, although this formula is not required. The guideline is suggested to give you a more comprehensive range of flavors choices in your herbal teas.

Using a fruity or naturally sweet part is excellent. A common choice here is dried rosehips. If you have not harvested your own, you can buy them in many shops that sell herbs or healthy food stores. Hibiscuses flowers are another option here, as they are lemony and sweetly flavored but they will also give a rich, red hue to your teas. Use these on the part of the fruity herbs.

Add in an herb to use for a place-holding flavor. This herb will bring the flavor that will hold all of the other flavors all together.  It will also make your iced tea with enough strong taste to stand up to the melting of a few cubes of ice. Use either red raspberry leaves that are dried first or nettles that are dried for this application. Use two parts of flavor holding herbs.

Especially useful for iced tea in the summer, an herb that cools is a perfect ingredient. Mint is the herb used the most commonly here. You can blend in any variety or combination of available mint flavor herbs you have. Another herb that is naturally cooling that will work well to complete your blend is the herb borage—the flowers or leaves or both of them can be used. Add in one part cooling herbs to complement your recipe.

Every essential blend will include notes of a flowery herb of some sort. Standard choices will include flower petals from violets, flowers of the chamomile plant, petals from dandelions, petals from the calendula plant, or petals from the wild rose. Add in one part of this herb.

This recipe is a recipe for an anti-anxiety blend that will leave you feeling relaxed and soothed. When you are creating a recipe, one part is the same measurement for each item. One component might be a teaspoon, a cup, or a gallon.

Tranquility Tea

Four parts chamomile
Two parts rose petals
Two parts lemongrass

Mix these three herbs all together in a jar made of glass and shake this jar to mix the spices. To make a cup of Tranquility Tea, add one teaspoon of the mix to a strainer or a loose tea ball and steep the herbs by covering them with freshly boiling water for five to ten minutes. Use honey for sweetness if you wish.

Stress Relief Tea

Two parts dried holy basil
One part dried lemon balm
One part dried chamomile
One part dried lavender
One part dried eleuthero root

# Aromatherapy

The scents of various items can be used to improve your mood or health. These operate by activating the receptors for smell inside your nose, sending subtle messages out to the nervous system. They may also make a slight effect in the energetic systems in your body. Aromatherapy is considered to be a natural remedy to relieve stress and anxiety. Before using them applied to the skin, essential oils definitely must be diluted by using the carrier oil. This dilution reduces your risk of irritation. A good rule is to dilute fifteen drops of your choice of essential oil with one ounce of the carrier oil. Some favorite carrier oils you can use are almond, jojoba, and coconut.

Essential oils are created from parts of trees, herbs, and flowers. You will use the roots, peels, bark, and petals. The fragrant smell of a plant is the essence, and this is from where essential oils come. When you extract meaning from a plant, the essence becomes an essential oil. Natural essential oils are not blended with other chemicals or fragrances. They are made using a specific process that does not change the chemistry of the plant. Smell receptors in your brain are activated during aromatherapy, and these receptors send messages to your brain through your nervous system. Your limbic system plays a role in your emotions. Your hypothalamus also works to produce good feelings in your body.

Fennel is a cooking spice with an aroma like licorice and it will treat most of the side effects of anxiety, especially the issues involving digestion. It can even help relieve the pressure that is usually related to menopause and some other conditions. Fennel supplements the side effects of stress. It is not quite clear if inhaling the fennel will give you the same impact, but it is always worth trying. Add in some diluted essential oil of fennel to your warm bath when you need to relax.

Lemon balm will give you a fresh aroma that is uplifting. In the practice of aromatherapy, it gives you a soothing, therapeutic effect. Capsules made from lemon balm might help some people that have moderate forms of anxiety disorders. It might also help you improve your sleep. Lemon balm in the diffuser will scent the entire room. You can even inhale it.

Patchouli is a musky scent that will work to relieve the effects of depression, stress, and anxiety. Combine patchouli with some of the other mild essential oils like some lavender. Patchouli promotes peace and relaxation. Inhale patchouli oil directly to relieve pressure or add a few drops to a warm bath or room diffuser.

Clary sage definitely is not the same common food herb you use in your stuffing recipes at holiday meals. The herbal, woody scent is excellent for calming stress and anxiety. This herb will ease your tension and will help you to control your cortisol levels, the stress hormone. When you feel anxious, you can inhale clary sage oil directly or rub it into your skin.

A peaceful scent is the essential oil extracted from rose petals. Use a basin filled with warm water, adding in a few drops of rose essential oil, to soak your feet. Some people add rose essential oil to a favorite unscented moisturizer to massage into the skin.

Chamomile is prized for its relaxing properties and intoxicating scent. People who suffer from anxiety that is mild to moderate may want to use Chamomile supplements. Add chamomile to a warm bath or rub a few drops onto your wrists or temples.

The beautiful flowery aroma of oil of jasmine can give you a sense of peace and calm. Unlike some of the other essential oils that will cause drowsiness when used for anxiety, jasmine essential oil does not. Use jasmine essential oil in your bath, put a few drops into a diffuser, or inhales the scent directly from the bottle.

Lavender essential oil calms the part of the brain that controls your emotions. Mix several drops of lavender oil directly into your bath water to enjoy a soothing bath before bed. Lavender essential oil is relaxing and will make you sleepy.

Valerian is another herb used since ancient times to promote peace and calm. The essential oil has a mild sedative effect on your body. Inhale the scent of valerian directly to feel sleepy or relaxed.

Jatamansi comes from the valerian plant family. It has been prominent in ancient medicine for centuries to encourage sleep. Massage diluted jatamansi essential oil into your forehead or temples.

Tulsi, or holy basil, is not the same kind of basil you use when you are making your lasagna, although it is from the same food family. The compound that gives holy basil the spicy, minty aroma has shown great promise in the treatment of physical and mental stress. This herb has a powerful fragrance, so you only need to use a few drops for an excellent effect. Use holy basil in an aromatherapy diffuser and breathe in the scent as the aroma floats around throughout the room.

Bergamot essential oil is made from bergamot oranges. The refreshing scent of citrus will help relieve your feelings of anxiety and elevate your mood. Carry bergamot oil with you at all times by placing a few drops onto a handkerchief and breathe in the scent two or three times when you need to relieve anxiety.

Vetiver might be lesser known than some of the other essential oils, but it is no less significant. The grassy vetiver plant native to India creates vetiver oil. The sweet earthy aroma is used in aromatherapy to promote relaxation. Rub it into your skin after diluting.

Flowery-scented ylang-ylang can be used in aromatherapy to increase feelings of relaxation. Breathing in a blend of ylang-ylang that is mixed with lavender and bergamot will lower stress and anxiety levels as well as your blood pressure and your heart rate. Apply drops of diluted ylang-ylang onto your skin, add it into a room diffuser, or breathe it in directly.

Frankincense oil is known by its sweet musky aroma that is felt to reduce anxiety. Aromatherapy that uses a blend of frankincense along with some lavender and bergamot will definitely improve your anxiety along with your depression and pain. Rub it directly on your feet just before bed.

Geranium plants create geranium essential oil, which can help reduce anxiety when diluted. Apply the geranium essential oil directly to a cotton ball and wiggle it around under your nose for a few minutes.

Sweet marjoram is also known as oregano, and the essential oil is often used to calm anxiety and nervousness. It is also often used to ease the pain of headaches, which are a commonly felt symptom of anxiety. Rub a few drops of diluted scent directly onto your wrists or temples, or add it to a diffuser.

# Chapter 7: The Six Steps To Calm

Everyone has feelings of fear or anxiety at some time in their lives. You might worry about your teenager out driving around at night. You might fret wondering about whether you will be let go from work. You will fear the absolute worst possible outcome if you notice a strange lump or feel a weird pain. Your worst fears will probably never happen, and that is the bizarre reality of anxiety. Your teen driver arrives safely home. There is no feared pink slip with your paycheck. And the lump you found is ruled to be of no real concern.

Life is full of little unknowns. Your body is hard-wired to jump directly into its feelings of fear when it feels as though its very survival is being threatened. Few people among you can calmly wait and tolerate the big "what ifs" that will enter your thoughts almost every day. Since you are not able to control those things that pop into your brain, you need to learn ways in which to control how you react to those body changing sensations and those anxious feelings and thoughts.

While it is perfectly normal to feel nervous about a significant event in your life or a change, many people live every day suffering with an anxiety disorder. This feeling is more than just the occasional bouts with worry or fear. An anxiety disorder can be as mild as generalized anxiousness over nothing to more substantial generalized anxiety where you worry over everything. It can even lead to a specific form of the disorder that causes intense panic attacks.

Those with an anxiety disorder need to use various strategies to help them reduce or eliminate their anxiety over the longer term, like forms of talk therapy or perhaps some medication. Anyone with the fear of any kind will benefit from some other methods to reduce their levels of stress and anxiety. An excellent place to begin is making specific lifestyle changes. Eat a healthy diet, limit your intake of alcohol and caffeine, and take some time for you.

There are also some steps that you can use in those moments when anxiety tries to gain hold. Use these suggestions from the experts to help to relax your mind and also to help you regain the control of your emotions.

**You need to accept your anxiety and release the emotions you hold regarding the concern**. It may sound counterintuitive, but getting your stress will help you feel less anxious instead of feeling ashamed or frustrated by it. It does not matter whether your anxiety came from your family or your lifestyle, or a combination of both. The pressure is here now, and when you acknowledge it instead of fighting it, that will free you to learn ways to manage it. Accepting the fact that you have anxiety does not mean giving up, either. You will stop spending valuable energy berating yourself for having anxiety and instead spend time learning what works for you to enable you to self-serve.

Emotions show up physically — pure energy that is put out by your brain. When you feel emotions, you also feel those physical symptoms like shortness of breath, rapid heartbeat, or an upset stomach. You might physically and constructively let go of fear by shivering and quivering like a dog does when he is at the vet. Allow your whole body to do what it needs to do and let it wiggle and tremble. Do this with energy and vigor, and also put it accompanied by sounds and you will quite quickly see that your fears are eliminated.

Stand up straight, pull your shoulders back, and open your chest, and then breathe deeply for immediate relief from anxiety. Combining this posture with deep breathing will help your body remember that you are in no danger right now and that your body is in control and not helpless. If you can't stand up, square your shoulders back and pull open your chest. The essential thing is to stop hunching forward and to breathe deeply.

**Restore your perspective regarding your anxiety.** Think consciously to stop those repeating thoughts that are full of fear going around inside your head. You are in charge, and everything will be fine. Tell yourself these things are true, and that you will turn this around by thinking and acting positively. Keep stopping the old ideas and remember what is real.

When you are anxious, you are often caught in a negative thought loop. Play this game with yourself to get back into your body and stop anxiety fast:

- Name five things that you can see.
- Name five things that you can hear.
- Move five parts of your body.

**Look inside yourself for the answer.** Fear is usually something your mind made up that requires no response on your part. Sometimes, you can get rid of the anxiety and the physical feelings by stopping and asking yourself what it thinks needs to be done. Ask your heart if there is any action needed right now, and then listen.

Lavender oil is loaded with healing properties. It supports deep, restful sleep and promotes a feeling of calm. It can even help ease your headaches. Reduce your anxiety by keeping a bottle of lavender oil at your desk or in your purse if you have one. Smell the aroma or rub it into your temples when you need some calm and peace. You get bonus points for combining the sniffing with deep, even breaths. Exercise is also a definite way to reduce anxiety. In addition to

135

boosting your level of hormones that promote happiness, a brisk walk will clear your mind. It gets you breathing more deeply again since stress is intimately linked to shallow breathing.

**Make a list of those things that need attention.** Usually, fear is a sign that your life needs attention. Make a list on paper of all the things you want to do and all your biggest priorities. You will likely find that the feelings you are experiencing have nothing to do with the things you need to do. You might say you are worried about your financial future, but you have not finished the last class to attain your college degree. Having a degree would create up new opportunities for your career and end some of your financial concerns. Look over the list, put the items in order of priority, and then tackle one thing at a time.

**Do not globalize your fears, but stay on one specific topic.** When you let worry control you, then you usually end up worrying about everything. For example, you are not able to pay one bill for this month, and now suddenly your fear writes a novel about you getting tossed out of your home and turning into a homeless person with no family. Work on just one issue at a time, like that bill, and think of it as the one matter that needs your attention right now. Think of it as a challenge to your creativity and let your fear take a backseat.

If you have a panic attack, and you feel that your heart is racing, it is easy to believe some fatality is about to happen. Give this feeling a new name instead of buying into it. Remind yourself that this is just a panic attack, like the ones you have had before, and that it will eventually pass.

Do something constructive. Straighten up the items on your desk. Make a snack and take it back to your desk. Walk outdoors and pick a flower to smell, whichever one looks the best. Doing some form of action will interrupt your thought pattern, which is often where anxiety starts. Contact someone else and talk about your fears with them. Saying your fears out loud to another person can help you clearly see what they really are. You might also feel better if you write your concerns on paper.

**Encourage yourself regularly.** Keep offering yourself praise for each little step. Giving you this recognition will feel like a little victory. This victory is what strength and courage feels like; it feels like you are overcoming, being strong, and pushing your way through. You will grow more fearless every time.

Remember to stay loyal and faithful to your heart with every decision you make to manage and push through the fear. If any action you take along the way does not feel right, then do not do it. Your heart will make sure you know where to go. When you think you are missing the messages from your heart, take care of the feeling of fear in your physical body, shiver and shake, and listen again!

This final tactic might sound silly, but it is probably the most enjoyable one you will do. Watch videos of you're a comedian you like or funny television show. Laughter is really good medicine for a mind filled with anxiety. Laughter will definitely benefit your mental health; humor will help lower your stress as well as exercise can.

# Conclusion

Thank you for making it through to the end of *How To Be Calm: How to Stop the Anxiety and Live a Calm Life*; let's hope it was informative and give you all of the needed tools to achieve your goals, whatever they may be.

The next step is to address the anxiety that is holding you back. Stress is nothing to be ashamed of. As you learned in this book, no one is born with fear. It is something that you acquire from the events in your life. Everyone has a unique collection of events in their lives, some good and some bad, and all of these events will leave a mark on your mind and your soul. Those people who have experienced more threatening events than good ones will likely end up with some amount of anxiety in their adult lives.

This collection of bad events led to the anxiety you suffer from today. You might recall some of the events, but it is just as likely that you have no conscious memory of what happened to you. You can get rid of the ill effects leftover from those bad events by taking charge of your life if you want to.

In this book, you learned what anxiety is, how it will affect your life, and the causes of stress. There is also a section on different methods to reign in your life's anxiety and how to control its

139

effects. You do not need to let fear remain in charge. You can be in control of your life once again. You will no longer need to be a victim of anxiety. Take a walk, smell some flowers, or imagine a beautiful peace-filled place in your life. There are things that you can implement to relieve your stress and take control once again of your life once again.

Remember, having anxiety is nothing to be ashamed of, but refusing to address it gives up and allows fear to run your life. Stress no longer needs to control you. Take your life back and send anxiety on its way. Pay attention to the steps for becoming calm, as this will give you concrete ideas for dealing with a panic attack. There are ways to diminish the effects on your life.

Finally, if you found this book useful in any way, a review on Amazon is always appreciated!